The Truth About *Pygmalion*

HIS MAJESTY'S THEATRE
HERBERT TREE
PYGMALION

The Truth About
Pygmalion

RICHARD HUGGETT

Random House  New York

Manufactured in the United States of America by The Haddon Craftsmen, Inc., Scranton, Pennsylvania

First American Edition

23456789

To Joyce and Margery Weiner

ACKNOWLEDGEMENTS

THREE YEARS OF RESEARCH HAVE gone into this book and into the play from which it springs. The work has been intermittent but concentrated, and crammed into the intervals between my acting jobs in theatre, television and film studios. A great many people have supplied me with information and photographs and I would like to pay grateful tribute to them . . . to the only surviving members of the original *Pygmalion* company, Mr Basil Dean and Miss Margaret Bussé, to Mr George Nash and Mr Tony Lathom of the Gabrielle Enthoven Collection who placed at my disposal Tree's press-cuttings where I found the bulk of the material, to Paul Myer of the Lincoln Centre Theatre Museum, to Mrs Olive Ripman, who produced Edmund Gurney's scrapbook, and to Mr John Merivale, who performed a similar service with *his* father's scrapbook, to Mr Alan Dent, whose two books the biography of Mrs Pat and his edition of her letters to Shaw, were my constant companions, to Mr Charles Landstone, Mr Harald Melville, the late Anthony Asquith, Miss Marie Löhr, Miss Ellen Pollock, Mr Robert Andrews, Mr David Tree and Mr Patrick Beech. I must thank all those who wrote to me from all over the world in response to my appeals for information, too many to acknowledge separately, though I cannot omit the enormously helpful testimony of Mr John Smythe of California, Mr James Johnstone of New York and Miss Elfrida Cloete of Cape Town.

I thank also the Society of Authors as Agent for the Shaw Estate, Victor Gollancz Ltd, and The *Observer*, The *Daily Sketch* and The *Daily Express* for permission to quote.

Thanks are also due to Messrs Raymond Mander and Joe Mitchenson for their help in supplying some of the illustrations, to Mr Herbert Bray and Mr Frederick Workman of L.E.A. and to Mrs Keep of the Victoria and Albert Museum for helping with the cartoons in Tree's album.

I would like to extend grateful thanks to Mrs Edith Baxter and her family of the Holmesdale Hotel, Billingham, who provided me with the loving care and comfort which made the writing of this book so enjoyable, and finally to Miss Rachel Montgomery, my editor at Heinemann, who guided me so painlessly and pleasantly through the pre-publication jungle.

The following photographs were supplied by courtesy of:
Lilli Marberg as Eliza, Vienna, 1913 (Raymond Mander and Joe Mitchenson Theatre Collection). Tilla Durieux as Eliza, Berlin, October 1913 *(The Sphere)*. Mrs. Patrick Campbell *(The Sketch)*. Mrs. Pat with Stella, Henry Ainley, Lady Randolph Churchill and George Cornwallis-West *(The Tatler)*. Mrs. Pat as Eliza *(Sporting and Dramatic News)*. Scenes from *Pygmalion*, 1914 (Raymond Mander and Joe Mitchenson Theatre Collection). Edmund Gurney as Doolittle (Mrs. Olive Ripman). Cartoons appearing after *Pygmalion* première (Photo: Malcolm Keep). Cartoons of the first cast of *Pygmalion* (Photos: Malcolm Keep). George Bernard Shaw *(Illustrated London News)*. Mrs. Pat as Eliza 1920 (Thomson Newspapers Ltd.). His Majesty's Theatre about 1900 (From the Mansell Collection and the Raymond Mander and Joe Mitchenson Theatre Collection).

The Truth About *Pygmalion*

I

MRS PATRICK CAMPBELL DIED IN
1940 at the age of seventy-five in a dingy little hotel
in Pau, a town in the South of France, where she had
lived for the last year of her life. She had been one of
the greatest actresses of her day, adored, spoiled and
fêted over two continents, and she died alone, impoverished and virtually unmourned. In fact, she had
been dead in her bed for three days before another
English lady in the hotel thought to enquire after her
and forced the manager to investigate; the English
clergyman who buried her did not know who she
was.

Her life had been a dream fantasy; the real world
filled with real people was something she never understood. Her existence had brought little but em-
barrassment and frustration to those who had known
and loved her best; her death came as a relief, particularly to herself, for her last years had been anything but happy, condemned as she had been to
wander alone and virtually penniless through a succession of cheap hotels in London, New York and
Paris. Poverty is, of course, a relative term, and although she was to complain loud and long about it,
she was, in fact, better provided for than most people
realized. Benjamin Guinness and his wife, two old
friends, had given her an annuity of £500 a year,
which before the war would have been worth about
£2,000 in contemporary money. A single woman

might have lived comfortably on it with the exercise of a little care and economy, but these qualities were as alien as tact and discretion to her extravagant temperament. Generous friends, like Bernard Shaw, occasionally gave her money, but life for her was a perpetual struggle to make ends meet.

This struggle was no less heart- and spirit-breaking for being largely her own fault. If she could have managed her career a little more sensibly her final years would have been much easier. She did receive the occasional film offer, but she refused them all for a reason which made film producers in England throw up their hands in despair—she didn't wish to leave Moonbeam. This was a vile-tempered, evil-smelling, crapulous pekinese, the last in a long line of such animals who had enjoyed a similarly privileged position in her life. Lonely old women frequently make fools of themselves over their pets, and Mrs Pat was no exception. Moonbeam not only lived on the expensive foods she could scarcely afford, but received the full force of a passionate and generous temperament which could have been better lavished on others. When, in 1938, Anthony Asquith asked her to play Mrs Higgins in the film of *Pygmalion* and later the part of Lady Britomart in the film of *Major Barbara*, she declined. 'It's those *dreadful* quarantine laws,' she boomed in that rich, deep voice which even the Continental telephone service could not dim, 'how can I leave my darling Moonbeam for six months in one of those cold, horrible kennels where he'll have to associate with all those nasty, rough, common

2

dogs? *Too* horrible! To him I'm a goddess, he trusts me implicitly. How can I betray him? I'm sorry, Puffin darling, you'll just have to get somebody else.' She approved of Leslie Howard who was Asquith's choice for Higgins, 'so English, I adore that vague, tweedy charm . . . you'd never guess he was an Austrian Jew, would you?' and expressed polite interest in his choice for Eliza, 'I've never heard of her but I'm sure she'll be very, *very* good.' But nothing he could say, no money he could offer, could induce her to change her mind.

A typical Shavian blast of wrath swept across the channel over Moonbeam: 'For heavens sake, Stella,' he wrote, 'when that wretched animal is killed by an automobile or perishes in the course of nature, buy a giant panda or a giraffe or a water buffalo, any of which you can take anywhere.' Mrs Higgins and Lady Britomart were eventually played, and very well, by Marie Löhr.

In refusing these two parts she deprived herself of the hundreds of pounds which Gabriel Pascal would have paid her and which would have cushioned her declining years very comfortably, but undoubtedly posterity's loss is greater. Under Asquith's tactful direction and beautiful photography, her performances would have been a far greater and more revealing gift to posterity than any of her brief and unsatisfactory film appearances in Hollywood, which, badly directed and abominably photographed, give only the most fleeting glimpses of her quality. Perhaps Moonbeam's quarantine was only an excuse:

perhaps the real reason lay deeper—a reluctance to see any other actress play Eliza. She had never taken to talented young actresses in her company, and it is a matter of pure speculation as to how she would have behaved to Wendy Hiller, the film's Eliza. She might have decided to be nice to her and would have been helpful on the set and friendly off it. Perhaps— and more probably—she would have made her life a misery. Posterity will never know, for the film was made without her and enjoyed a spectacular success, though in her Continental exile she never lived to see it.

Throughout her last years she had one exceedingly valuable possession, a hat box containing Shaw's letters to her and hers to Shaw which at her request he had returned. Photostats of all of them had been deposited in a New York bank but the originals remained with her till her death and were then smuggled over to England by a friend. There had been a lot of trouble over those letters because an American publisher had offered her $20,000 for the publication rights, and in the last ten years she had made increasingly urgent attempts to persuade Shaw to allow her to publish them. But because Charlotte, his wife, was still alive and had never really cared for Mrs Pat (few wives did), Shaw had persistently refused. Underneath it all, he was an old-fashioned gentleman with a strong sense of marital honour and he did not wish to cause his wife any pain.

Mrs Pat continued to plead and her letters make painful reading. Shaw, his patience visibly wearing thin, continued to refuse. Mrs Pat pointed out, as many people did, that he had allowed his letters to Ellen Terry to be published, so why not his to herself? There were good reasons for this and he explained them at great length and the answer was still emphatically and irrevocably NO. But he sympathized with her troubles and as well as giving her money he also gave her some good financial advice. 'Write the true story of *Pygmalion*', he said, 'and you'll make all England and North America laugh uproariously. Hutchinsons will advance you a thousand pounds without winking. But mind, Stella, the dismal string of lies in your last letter is not worth twopence. It must be the utter, grotesque truth!'

The truth about *Pygmalion*, the utter, grotesque truth . . . As was fitting for such a supreme master of language, Shaw had chosen his adjectives with great care, for the truth was indeed grotesque, and much more besides. It was a thousand pities that neither he nor Mrs Pat lived to write it, for the events which filled the spring and summer of 1914 were rich in comedy and drama, and cast an intriguing light on some of the more bizarre aspects of theatrical behaviour. The rehearsals for *Pygmalion* and the scandal which followed the first performance provide a unique chapter in theatrical history, for it was over this play that Shaw, Mrs Pat and Sir Herbert Beerbohm Tree met and worked together for the first time in their careers. Here were three of the most monstrous egotists the theatre ever produced, all at the height of their talents and fame, all accustomed to getting their own way in everything without opposition, now meeting in headlong collision. Individually they were difficult enough, if not downright impossible; any two of them would have produced fireworks, but all three together working on the same play was theatrical dynamite. The ensuing explosion reverberated long and wide, and its echoes can still be faintly heard today, but out of it was born the masterpiece which the world knows and loves.

For each of them the play was a milestone in their lives. For Tree, *Pygmalion* was the final, exultant climax to a long and distinguished life in the theatre. For Mrs Pat, it was the crest of a wave which was soon to crash on to a hard and stony beach. For Shaw, it was a turning point which was to change him from being the darling of the intellectual coteries into a household word, for until 1914 he had enjoyed a strangely mixed, oddly ambiguous reputation. All over America and on the Continent, his plays were never off the stage, he was widely acclaimed as the greatest living playwright—particularly in Germany—and the combined royalties from the two continents had turned him into a very wealthy man. Gone were the days of genteel poverty when, as a young man, he had written his five unreadable novels in Fitzroy Square while his mother and sister supported him. Now he had a large country house and garden, a flat in London, a motor-car and a four-figure income.

But in England it was a very different story. It would, perhaps, be a slight exaggeration to say that the prophet was totally without honour, but the sad fact remained that the bulk of the British public regarded him with a mixture of suspicion and bewilderment. At the age of fifty-seven he was a strikingly controversial figure, known to all, hated by many, but adored by a select few. For this minority he could do no wrong, but the public at large found him baffling, infuriating, paradoxical, clownish and totally unpredictable. It is unlikely if anybody, before or since, had so mastered the sublime art of annoying the British public. He was serious about funny things and funny about serious things and the public didn't know what to make of him. Already he had not one but many careers behind him—political pamphleteer, novelist, art critic; a music critic who had achieved the miracle of making this esoteric stuff not merely intelligible to those who knew nothing about music but positively enjoyable; a dramatic critic who for three years had kept the West End theatre in general and the actor-managers in particular hopping with alarm and despondency; and finally he was a playwright who wrote plays which everybody agreed were not really plays at all, but merely endless conversational mouthpieces for his own unorthodox opinions; nevertheless, they had an uncanny knack of working theatrically and of getting themselves talked about. If the British public had been collectively asked to define its picture of Shaw in the spring of 1914, it would probably have been something like this: a vegetarian, a socialist, a street-corner orator who wore hand-woven Jaeger tweed suits, and whose obscene plays had been rightly banned by the Lord Chamberlain. In fact, only two of them had been refused a licence, *Mrs Warren's Profession* back in 1898 and *The Shewing-up of Blanco Posnet* in 1909, but the British public had always dearly loved a generalization.

Obscene or not, these plays were intellectual and full of social comment, and this—far more then than now—was fatal to the British box-office and deeply repellent to a public whose idea of an entertaining evening in the theatre was a tailor's advertisement making love to a milliner's advertisement in the middle of a designer's and upholsterer's advertisement. Eleven of them had been performed at the Royal Court Theatre under the Vedrenne-Barker management, and had drawn a select band of worshippers to the Shavian shrine, but when they travelled to the West End, the pilgrims who followed them made up in fanaticism what they lacked in numbers. Actors admired Shaw because he wrote such good parts; managers distrusted him because his plays invariably lost money even when they carried the insurance of star names—Sir Johnston Forbes-Robertson in all his glory was unable to save *Caesar and Cleopatra* at the Savoy from financial disaster. In twenty years, over a dozen of his best known plays had been produced, but none of them, not even the long-running *Fanny's First Play* had made money. In England, Shaw had never enjoyed one really big, spectacular, money-spinning success. As a result he had no time for the commercial theatre and the commercial theatre had no time for him. They lived in a state of reciprocal distrust and resentment, so by mutual consent they wisely steered clear of each other.

This was the situation in 1914 when *Pygmalion* was produced; overnight everything was changed, dramatically and irrevocably. Shaw went to bed and, like Byron, woke to find himself a legend, for by making a fashionable actress use bad language in a fashionable play in a fashionable theatre, he had become more famous than the Pope, the Kaiser, the King and the Archbishop of Canterbury.

★

The part of Eliza Doolittle was inspired by Mrs Patrick Campbell and written specially for her; since she is the focal point of this story, it is necessary to examine in some detail the background and per-sonality of this extraordinary woman. She was a phenomenon, and it is unlikely that theatrical history can produce anybody who was as dazzlingly gifted in so many different ways. She was beautiful with a blazingly dark-eyed, broodingly sexual beauty which aroused poets, painters and writers to a frenzy. Her acting ability was exceptional, amounting on oc-casions to genius which placed her overnight at the very top of her profession in an age already filled with great actresses—Ellen Terry, Duse, Réjane and Sarah Bernhardt were pleased to accept her as their equal. Her voice was warm, rich and deep like a cello, and although there are, unhappily, no records of it, there is abundant testimony to its thrilling and hypnotic quality; when old people speak mistily of her, it is her voice they remember first. 'You make an ugly language sound beautiful,' said Coquelin to her after he had seen her Ophelia. If Bernhardt's voice was likened to gold, then Mrs Pat's was purple and crimson flecked with silver. She was devastatingly witty in a period of history which was already filled with wits: her sayings were widely quoted, found their way into print and are now accepted as classics of their kind; she could even outshine Shaw and not many people were able to do that. She had a fascination and charm which was irresistible when she chose to exert it, and if all this wasn't enough, she could play the piano beautifully. She could have had a strikingly successful career as a concert pianist if she had chosen, and England's subsequent musical history might have been suitably enriched: but she chose otherwise, and music's loss was the theatre's gain. All in all, she was an arch-enchantress of a very rare and special sort, who fascinated her public and enslaved some of the greatest geniuses of her day. For the most part they went quietly, for no man could stand up to her for long if she chose to capture him.

She was born Beatrice Stella Tanner in 1865 of very mixed parentage. She was Italian on her mother's side, descended from a long line of minor and impoverished aristocracy, though her grandfather had actually descended to managing a circus and her mother to riding a horse in it. On her father's side she was English with a strong association with the

Protestant clergy. The Tanners had provided the Church of England with a praiseworthy selection of vicars, deans, canons and even a bishop or two. She was an odd mixture—part Venice, part suburban Dulwich. From the sun-drenched south, she derived her looks and the passionate impulsiveness of a wayward and unpredictable temperament, and from the cold north, she inherited an instinctive respectability and a strong streak of puritanism.

This last was her saving grace and something she urgently needed. Life was hard in the nineties for a young woman with two children living apart from her husband and with no family to protect her, and it was Mrs Pat's misfortune that she should have been born into an era when the theatre was struggling to achieve respectability above all else, and when it was automatically assumed that actresses were immoral. With Mrs Pat, these suspicions hardened into a certainty. With those passionate eyes, that sensual figure, that husky sexual voice which held promise of so many nameless erotic delights, how could one doubt that she was the visible incarnation of all those scarlet women who filled the fashionable literature of the day? And as for the women she impersonated, Paula, Sonia, Magda, Mrs Ebbsmith, Lady Macbeth, Hedda Gabler, Bella Donna, all of them abandoned women who tore off their clothes, threw bibles into the fire, sobbed their passions at the feet of impeccably dressed lovers, murdered their husbands or renounced them to live with Arabs in the desert, how could any sensible person doubt that she must have much in common with these hussies if she was able to portray them so convincingly?

Mrs Pat did little to undeceive them and there was an intriguing paradox in this. In fact, she was a perfectly respectable married woman with two children, and her private life was all that the most exacting Victorian moralist could wish, but only her friends knew this. The public might assume what it wished and Mrs Pat, with that imp of devilment which was always bubbling just under the surface, enjoyed letting them think the worst. In short she was playing a double game—subtly pretending to be wicked, in reality being good all the time, and this, as Oscar Wilde firmly pointed out, was Hypocrisy.

All her life she detested hypocrisy just as she detested the maiden name of Tanner. An early marriage when she was nineteen enabled her to discard it for ever, and it was this, as much as a desire for security, which prompted her to keep her married name when she started her professional career in the theatre. The habit of actresses retaining their married names, which added such a charmingly domestic touch to eighteenth- and nineteenth-century playbills, was on the decline. Mrs Pat was the last actress ever to do this.

Mr Patrick Campbell who, like *Mr* Siddons, *Mr* Beeton, *Mr* Kendal and *Mr* Gaskill, takes his place amongst the shadow-husbands of history, was a good-looking young man of undefined occupation and uncertain income—*gentleman of fortune* was the polite term in middle-class Victorian society. It was not a successful marriage, for she was temperamentally unsuited to close and permanent relationships; it was clear she was the sort of woman you just can't live with. Shaw sensibly realized this and did not try. 'I would not have lasted a week,' he said after her death. Mr Patrick Campbell endured it for just a little over three years and then fled to South Africa, preferring the rigours of the gold-mines with the Afrikaners in the Transvaal to domestic bliss with his beautiful but difficult wife in south London.

She started her professional career in 1888 at the age of twenty-five. Five years of hard, rigorous touring in the provinces followed and then in 1893 her sensational début at the St James's Theatre under George Alexander's management in Pinero's *The Second Mrs Tanqueray*. History was made, and she was a super-star, long before the term was invented. Naturally she had to behave like one, and for her this meant only one thing. No sooner had she read her notices, each one a love letter from the critics, than she started to assert herself in ways which few could forgive but which all were forced to tolerate. Stories began to circulate of her rudeness, her arrogance, her unreliability, her difficult conduct off the stage and her truly appalling behaviour on it. She became professionally such a nuisance that nobody who had ever been associated with her wished to repeat the experience if he could possibly avoid it. What was this imp of perversity which made her behave so badly so soon after her name was made? Somewhere deep down in that strangely complex personality was a terrifying instability, an almost suicidal neurosis which forced her to try and destroy what she had so carefully created. But try as she might, even she could not destroy such a brilliant career because for twenty years, while she was in her prime, she was unique and irreplaceable, and the theatre has always secretly loved its bitch-goddesses. She could behave as she did with impunity; she knew it and so did everybody else. Even George Alexander, a pompous, self-important, humourless man who was her chief victim, was compelled to offer her no less than six engagements, though each time the wretched, persecuted man swore it would be the last.

But nobody remains irreplaceable for ever, and in the fullness of time, Mrs Pat met her deserts. The First World War destroyed her world and with it the actor-managerial system which upheld it. She outlived her age, finding herself rejected and, finally, forgotten in the post-war years. Fat, ugly and ageing, a long professional decline was her fate, in which she was condemned to reviving her old parts with inferior companies in suburban theatres, and begging for work. Thanks to her, both Pinero and Shaw had enjoyed their greatest successes, but though they both wrote plays with parts which would have suited her to perfection and which were, in fact, tailor-made for her—Iris, Hesione, Orinthia, The Serpent—they both refused to employ her. It came to the point where nobody would give her work, and she was compelled to emigrate to Hollywood with all its horrors and humiliations. It was all very sad.

For all her intelligence and culture, Mrs Patrick Campbell was a very stupid woman. She had the world at her feet and the best she could do was to kick it far away from her into the gutter where even she could not reach it.

But all this is to anticipate. On that first glorious night at the St James's Theatre in 1893 it was tears, cheers, roses and champagne—and Bernard Shaw. This is where the story really starts for he was in the audience. Hers was, by all accounts, one of the most sensational débuts of the century. Nobody remotely like her had been seen before or was to be seen again. Not only had she put on the stage a new sort of woman, but she had almost succeeded in convincing the critics that Pinero had written a new sort of play. Only Shaw seemed to have realized that he hadn't— the model was fully sixty years old and dying on its feet, but Pinero, with the cunning of a veteran crafts-man, had neatly disguised the fact. Shaw was en-raptured with her, but it is typical of him that he should have announced that it was her piano playing and her physical dexterity which had impressed him most. 'She's unique,' he remarked to Pinero, 'not that she's a great actress, *but she can thread a needle with her toes*!' This must be taken with a large pinch of Shavian salt, for contradicting himself was a favourite hobby amounting to an occupational disease, which caused bewilderment to his contemporaries and con-fusion to his biographers. Whatever he said or wrote about Mrs Pat, the fact remained that Shaw had the greatest possible respect for her acting abilities.

During his three-year tenure as dramatic critic for *The Saturday Review*, he lavished the most eloquent praise on her best performances, and as further proof of his sincerity, when he started to write plays in 1892, he wanted her for many of his leading parts—Mrs Warren, Candida, Raina, Mrs Dubedat and Cleopatra. In fact, Cleopatra was the only one of these which she did play, and it was a single performance in Newcastle in 1899, hastily thrown together to establish the copyright.

In 1897 she joined Forbes Robertson's company at the Lyceum for a season of classical revivals. She played Ophelia to his Hamlet and Shaw noted with approval that in the mad scene she was truly, terrifyingly and astonishingly mad. Three months later he returned to see it a second time, but the production and all the performances had deteriorated badly. Mrs Pat was now thoroughly bored with Ophelia—'a very silly girl, she needed a good shaking,' was her comment—and instead of madness, now offered the stereotyped sentimental idiocy familiar to, and favoured by, the Victorian theatregoers. None of this would be worthy of attention or comment but for one interesting fact: it was this performance which, strangely enough, gave Shaw the first idea for *Pygmalion* though it was some fifteen years before he actually came to writing it. 'Caesar and Cleopatra have been driven clean out of my head by a play I wish to write for them in which he shall be a West End gentleman and she a flower-girl with an apron and three red ostrich feathers in her hat. Oooooh, she'll be a rapscallionly flower-girl!' Just what Mrs Pat was doing to make Shaw think of a flower-girl is not known, but apparently there was something in the way she sang and decked herself with flowers in the mad scene which reminded him irresistibly of the lady who sold flowers in Charing Cross station.

Shortly after this they were introduced to each other and proceeded to exchange their first cautious letters. 'My dear Mrs Patrick Campbell . . .' 'Dear Mr Shaw . . .' The tone was friendly, though the approach was formal, and with no hint of the raptures and agonies to come.

2

FIFTEEN YEARS PASSED DURING which time Shaw forgot all about his flower-girl and the lady who was to inspire her. Apart from a few casual, friendly letters, he and Mrs Pat had no communication with each other, each being busy with their separate careers. Shaw wrote *The Doctor's Dilemma*, *Man and Superman*, *You Never Can Tell*, *Getting Married*, *The Devil's Disciple* to name only a few. Mrs Pat toured America extensively and appeared in many long-since-forgotten plays, though her performance as Hedda Gabler was a major breakthrough for the unpopular, suspect Ibsen who, in spite of Shaw's championship, had not yet been accepted in England. Her husband was killed in the Boer war and her two children, Stella and Alan (known as Beo) both married and joined the profession, Stella as an actress—she was professionally known as Stella Patrick Campbell—and Beo as an actor and playwright.

Then in 1912 she played one of the last of her six engagements with the long-suffering George Alexander, now Sir George and a very dignified gentleman. This was an adaptation by Robert Hichens of his own highly popular novel, *Bella Donna*, a torrid, atmospheric romantic drama set in the Far East which provided yet another display of Mrs Pat's extraordinary ability to transform a thoroughly bad play into a hugely popular success. At the end she was required to ride into the desert, and into one of the St James's most spectacular sunsets, on a donkey, an intelligent animal who showed his good taste and judgement by loudly misbehaving on the first night. 'I *adored* that donkey,' Mrs Pat used to say fondly, 'he had such *beautiful* manners.'

Shaw went to see the play and in the interval paid Mrs Pat a visit backstage. It was a long-accepted tradition in the Victorian theatre for stars to receive visitors in the interval, a custom which was accepted much more readily than it is now. In those days because the scenery was so elaborate and required such frequent changing, the intervals were much longer. When Mrs Pat held court in her dressing-room, intervals were liable to be very long indeed; for her convenience, the play might be cut but never the intervals. While she was changing her costume they talked about the play. 'I hate it,' she moaned, 'it's so *crude*! Bella Donna is such a bad woman. People think I'm like that, even darling Robert Hichens does. I want to play nothing but *saints*, but they won't let me. Oh, she's an abominable woman.'

'Very appropriate,' said Shaw, '*Bella Donna* is an abominable play. I've never seen anything like it. If Sardou and David Belasco had collaborated they might conceivably produce something like this. The only thing to be done with it is to set it to music. Somebody ought to invite Puccini. However, you're the only actress in London who could make sense out of it; it's certainly a pleasure to hear a beautiful voice. How did you get it, I've often wondered?'

'God gave it to me,' she replied smiling.

'I have only one criticism. You speak English better than anyone else in the English theatre, but it is too careful. I repeatedly find myself listening to the voice and not to the words. That may be all right for Patti but it really won't do for Mrs Pat who's worth ten of her.'

Mrs Pat was not slow to accept this challenge. 'Will you write a play for me? Will you write your *next* play for me?' Shaw agreed. 'Then write me a cockney part,' she said with a touch of defiance, 'and I'll show you what I can do. I'm much more versatile than people suspect. I'm so tired of playing ladies. Give me something nice and common, there's a dear.' Shaw nodded and went to see Alexander who was evidently thinking along the same lines as his leading lady. 'Why don't you write a play for me, Mr Shaw?' he said. '*Bella Donna* won't last for ever and I really do need a new play for the autumn.'

It had been a fateful day, for out of those two short conversations, *Pygmalion* was born. Shaw was a very quick worker and within a month the play was complete. Its literary antecedents are interesting. The legend of the sculptor who falls in love with his own statue has been used in one form or other for centuries; Plautus, Chaucer, Voltaire, W. S. Gilbert all wrote plays on the theme, but when *Pygmalion* was produced in Berlin, a German critic immediately recognized the plot as having been drawn from an incident in Smollett's novel, *Peregrine Pickle*. When Shaw was questioned about this, he irritably admitted having read the work in his Dublin boyhood but not since. His memory was evidently a good one for the plot follows Smollett's little romance very closely. In Chapter 87, Peregrine meets a sixteen-year-old beggar-girl in the road. She wears rags, her face is dirty and she talks the language of Billingsgate, but she has agreeable features. He buys her for a small sum from her mother, takes her home, gets his valet to give her a good scrubbing and rinsing, cuts her hair and gives her some attractive clothes to wear. He then proceeds to cure her of swearing, a most difficult task, and in a few weeks is able to present her at the table of a country squire, where she says very little but behaves well enough to provoke no comment. She goes to London and lives in private lodgings with a female attendant; she is instructed in dancing and French and attends plays and concerts several times a week. One evening while at cards, she detects a certain lady in the act of cheating; she swears violently and soundly cuffs her to the astonishment of all present. Nay, to such an unguarded pitch is she provoked that starting up, she snaps her fingers in testimony of disdain, and, as she leaves the room, applies her hand to that part of her which is the last to leave, and, referring to it by one of its coarsest denominations *invites the company to kiss it*! Peregrine finds himself spurned by society for this little escapade and is greatly relieved when the girl runs off with his valet; he gives them money to start a tavern.

Shaw called at the St James's Theatre and, as was his custom, read the play aloud to Alexander, his wife and his advisors. Shaw was a superb actor and he read his own plays magnificently, far better than many professional actors, which was sometimes inclined to have a discouraging effect on their performances. Alexander was not in the least discouraged: he was radiantly, boundlessly, hugely delighted. 'It's a cert, a dead cert,' he shouted. Then his face fell into unusually hard and determined lines. 'Now listen to me, Mr Shaw,' he said, 'I'll get you any actress you like to play Eliza and I'll pay her any salary she asks, you can settle your own terms. But go on for another play with Mrs Campbell, I will NOT!! I'd rather die.'

She was behaving very badly just then, much worse than usual. She had recently started the abominable habit of actually laughing outright on the stage during Alexander's scenes while he was trying to make love to her. *Bella Donna* was one of his rare excursions into character acting; he was playing an Eastern Jewish doctor in a fez, with a complexion and accent to match. 'My dear, you should see him,' Mrs Pat laughed with Shaw one day, 'his *voice*, his *face*, he looks and sounds just like my Swedish masseuse.' One day, Alexander's dresser called at her dressing-room and spoke very pompously to her. 'Sir George says please will you not laugh at him when he is on the stage.' Mrs Pat looked calmly at the man and replied: 'Please tell Sir George that he is greatly mistaken; I always wait until I get home before I laugh.' But whatever strained relations existed between Alexander and Mrs Pat, his conditions were impossible.

At that point Shaw had no strong views on the casting of Professor Higgins, but there was simply no question of anybody else in the West End playing Eliza. He had promised his next play to Mrs Pat, he had given his word, and whatever his other shortcomings might be, Shaw always kept his promises. When all was said and done, he was a gentleman.

It was this decision which now placed a curious diplomatic problem on his hands. Somehow he had to acquaint Mrs Pat with the play and obtain her approval of the part. But how? He realized that when she had expressed a desire to play a cockney part, what she had in mind was something rather genteel like Madame Sans-Gêne, the laundress who had been Ellen Terry's solitary excursion into the lower orders; or perhaps a lady's maid or shop assistant like the parts which Nancy Price was then playing so successfully, something well-dressed and clean which involved only the slightest distortion of those beautiful vowel sounds. But a flower-girl, a guttersnipe with a dreadful accent which you could hardly understand, using the most disgusting language never before heard on the stage, dirty with a lifetime's accumulated grime, crawling with fleas, and wearing rags so filthy that they had to be burned, never in her wildest dreams could she have anticipated this. How could he offer it to her with the explanation that, being a splendid ladies' tailor, the part fitted her as closely as Lady Cicely in *Captain Brassbound's Conversion* fitted Ellen Terry? Mrs Pat was a grand lady and accustomed to very grand parts; her rages were well known to be truly terrifying and even Shaw's courage failed him at the prospect. 'I simply didn't dare offer it to her,' he wailed to Ellen Terry. But a solution presented itself; the Hon. Mrs Edith Lyttleton, a close friend of theirs, known to them both as D.D., offered her services. Let Shaw read it to her, and let it be cunningly contrived that Mrs Pat should also be present, so that hearing the play should seem to be by mere chance.

'There's no point in my giving her the play to read for herself,' he said irritably. 'She doesn't know how to read a play, no actress does. She'll just look at her part and ignore the rest, I *know*, and that would be the end. No, the only chance we have is to get her interested in the play as a whole and then she'll beg to play Eliza. You'll see.'

It was quickly arranged. Mrs Lyttleton invited both of them to tea at her house at 16 Great College Street, Westminster; the date was June 26th and it was a fine summer's day. Mrs Pat arrived after a matinée at the theatre, 'reeking from *Bella Donna*', and full of backstage gossip. Conversation over the teacups tinkled along merrily until Mrs Pat noticed the manuscript lying on the table on Shaw's right. 'What's that?' she enquired, 'your new play?' Shaw nodded. 'Just a bit of nonsense I've written for Robert Loraine for his next tour.' Mrs Pat glared. 'You promised your next play would be for *me*! Your promises are like pie-crusts, Mr Shaw, and sorry ones at that.' Shaw nodded, smiling. 'And so it will,' he said, 'I'll write something really good for you.

This is only a pot-boiler, you wouldn't like this.' Mrs Pat picked up the manuscript and examined it. All seemed to be going to plan. 'I was going to read it to D.D.' said Shaw carelessly, 'but I won't bother, you wouldn't be interested.' But now Mrs Pat was very interested. 'I'd like to hear a bit of it,' she said, purring with malicious delight at the prospect of playing her favourite indoor game—humiliating authors who had written plays and wished to read them aloud in her presence; old or young, novices or veterans, it didn't matter because she was a past-mistress at the art of dealing with presumption. Henry Arthur Jones, who had a very strong cockney accent, once attempted to read a play to her; at the end she drawled out, 'Thank you, Mr Jones, but it's far too long, even without the aitches!' Clearly she would have to find another method of dealing with this imposing, beautifully-spoken Irishman; all un-suspecting, she reclined on the chaise-longue, Shaw took up the manuscript and, in an atmosphere of delicately-wrought tension, the reading began.

'*Pygmalion*, a romance in five acts. Act One, the portico of St Paul's Church, Covent Garden. It is raining, cab whistles are blowing frantically in all directions . . .' It was two months since he and Mrs Pat had last met; she had evidently forgotten their conversation for she had no inkling at this point that this was the play which Shaw had promised to write for her. For a time she listened with a slightly bored air, and when Shaw came to Eliza's first cry, 'Aa-ow-ooh,' she saw her chance and took it. 'Oh please, Mr Shaw,' she drawled with a pained expression on her face, 'not that unpleasant noise; it's not nice.'

For once, the game didn't work. After twenty years of working in the professional theatre, Shaw was well accustomed to leading actresses and their nonsense, and it took more than Mrs Pat to disconcert him. He ignored her and continued the reading. Presently he repeated the noise much louder, '*Aaaaah-ow-oooh*!!' Mrs Pat still had no suspicion that this was to be *her* part and that these two dreadful sounds would one day emerge from *her* throat. 'No, no, no, Mr Shaw,' she protested, a little more firmly this time. 'you really must not make that horrible sound again. It's vulgar!' But a terrible suspicion was beginning to form in her mind . . . could this be? . . . was it? . . . did he *seriously*? . . . was it possible . . . ? Shaw continued to ignore her, but when he repeated it worse than ever before, '*Aaaaaaaah-ow-ohh*!!!' trumpeting it at the top of his voice for all Westminster to hear, then suspicion ripened to a certainty. 'You beast,' she stormed, rising from the chaise-longue and confronting him, 'you wrote this play for *me*! I can actually hear you imitating my voice in every line of it!' Of course she was quite right; Shaw was a devastatingly accurate mimic and he was determined that Mrs Pat should guess the truth without being prompted. They all laughed heartily, Mrs Pat returned to her chaise-longue and Shaw continued the reading in silence.

She listened intently, nodding and smiling as the

comedy developed in ways which appealed to her, and breaking into open laughter during the tea-party scene. Her taste in drama was not infallible but she could recognize quality when she saw it, and Eliza was a superb part . . . but a flower-girl? For *her*? Reassurance came at the end of the play. She was required to speak cockney and to be unwashed only in two acts, and for the remaining three she could be as clean, well-dressed and as ladylike as she pleased. At the end of the reading she had made up her mind to do it, and when Shaw had finished she knew how to rise to the occasion. 'I am deeply flattered, Mr Shaw,' she intoned in that darkly thrilling voice which had enslaved two continents; and, as befits a famous actress being gracious to a distinguished author, she thanked him for the privilege he had extended to her in reading his beautiful play and offering her the leading part. She returned to the theatre for the evening performance leaving Shaw and Mrs Lyttleton to congratulate themselves on what had been, they hoped, a very satisfactory afternoon's work.

Reassurance arrived speedily next day. Mrs Pat sent Shaw a charmingly business-like letter of appreciation in which she thanked him for reading the play and wondered if, in playing his pretty slut, she might please him. She asked about dates and theatres and actors and invited Shaw to call and see her to discuss what she laughingly described as business. He did not need a second invitation. All unsuspecting, he called at 33 Kensington Square, fully intending to drive a bargain as hard as nails, but things turned out a little differently. Mrs Pat had decided to enslave him and she succeeded in doing precisely that. She brought into play all her formidable arsenal of charm, flattery, wit and femininity and succeeded in making him fall hopelessly in love in a record time of thirty seconds. Shaw made no resistance; he fell in love, head over ears, and dreamed and dreamed, and walked on air all that day and all the next as if he were once more an adolescent boy. The sirens sang a very sweet song on that hot summer's day, June 28th, 1912. 'I could think of nothing,' he wrote in a rapturous letter to Ellen Terry, 'except a thousand scenes in which she was the heroine and I the hero.' For a married man of fifty-six this was hardly fitting conduct—had he not already enjoyed a long series of love affairs with beautiful and successful women? But this was different: history has recorded few infatuations so ridiculous—or so delicious.

The following day, the spell was stronger than ever. Hand in hand, the old greybeard and the raven-haired enchantress, who was ten years his junior, wandered round London, exploring it like tourists, and finding and seeing it for the first time, as is the way with lovers. They drove through the parks in a taxi, paid calls on Mrs Pat's titled friends and exchanged lovers' nonsense on her sofa. His years fell from him like an old suit of clothes. He was in love with Mrs Pat for nearly two days, and for that experience, let all her sins be forgiven her. 'Many thanks for Friday and a Saturday of delightful dreams,' he wrote to her over the weekend. 'I am all right now . . . but it would be meanly cowardly to pretend that you are not a very wonderful lady or that the spell did not work most enchantingly on me for fully twelve hours.'

The afterglow was an Indian summer which lasted for more than a year and which overflowed into a series of love letters whose rapturous eloquence is without parallel in modern literature. They make fascinating reading, coming as they did from an intellectual who scorned romantic love as a foolish dream; but in these letters he wasn't in love as he had been with Ellen Terry, he was infatuated, and the giant had never looked more foolish. It was Mrs Pat who kept her head, for closer acquaintance with Shaw revealed unsuspected levels in his infinitely complex character. Underneath the arrogant confidence there was a shy provincial boy, and underneath that there was a compulsive exhibitionist. She had always been an astute judge of character and it was about this time that she gave him the nickname which she used for the rest of their lives—Joey. This was what circus people had traditionally called the clown with the white face and spangled costume, and this, she realized, was what Shaw really was—a brightly painted clown turning cartwheels in the spotlight and begging for applause. So Joey he became and Joey he stayed, though this was used only in letters and in private meetings. In the presence of others she called him Bernard, when she was in a good temper, Mr Shaw when she was not. Shaw was delighted to be called Joey. 'It was by far the cleverest thing you ever invented,' he later said to her.

But she wasn't so clever when it came to *Pygmalion*, as he quickly discovered. She loved the part and was anxious to start rehearsals immediately, in September if possible. So far so good; but there were many rocks and storms ahead and it was nearly two years before *Pygmalion* appeared in London. Many unexpected troubles contributed to this long delay, like the casting of Professor Higgins which turned out to be a great deal more difficult than anybody could ever have suspected. Mrs Pat, getting down to business sternly and brusquely, wanted to present the play under her own management, which would be greatly to her financial advantage, and with a leading man of her own choice. This would naturally be a competent, reliable, secondary actor who would do as she told him and who would not outshine her. But on this point her judgement was at fault: although she had been a star in the West End for twenty years, she sadly miscalculated her own drawing power and the specialized demands of the West End public. Shaw knew better: out of the depths of his theatrical wisdom he knew that although the single star system worked admirably in the provinces and in America, no star had ever been able to hold out in London for long. Barry Sullivan, Edward Terry, Ellen Terry, Robert Loraine, even Mrs Pat herself, had all tried and failed. It was always the combination which succeeded, as he firmly pointed out to her—Irving and Ellen Terry, Wyndham and Mary Moore, Julia Neilson and Fred Terry, Alexander and Irene Vanbrugh.

Mrs Pat questioned this and suggested a series of quite impossible people. Shaw was anxious to have Robert Loraine who had played Tanner very successfully in *Man and Superman* on an extended American tour and was one of his favourite actors. Mrs Pat didn't want him ('you can't be serious, him!!??'), but Shaw pressed his choice; so Mrs Pat gave her opinion of Robert Loraine in highly unflattering terms ('he's so dull that when he's alone on the stage it's empty—I can't stand the shape of his nose!'). This brought Shaw's imp of devilment to the surface; he repeated what she had said to an astonished and indignant Loraine who replied by saying equally unpardonable things about Mrs Pat ('woman's an amateur, doesn't know a dam' thing about acting, ought to be back in her grandfather's circus'). Shaw lost no time in repeating all this to Mrs Pat, who was not amused. 'You're a mischief-maker, Joey,' she stormed, so he obligingly went away and made some more. For a time it looked as if his tactics were going to work; Mrs Pat and Loraine were at last persuaded to meet to discuss the matter and to everybody's astonishment found themselves actually assuring each other of their undying esteem and mutual admiration, which was what Shaw had wanted in the first place. Unhappily, Loraine was facing another financial crisis and found himself compelled to return to America to supermanage himself into a solvent condition, so all talk of their doing *Pygmalion* together was postponed indefinitely. Mrs Pat continued to be difficult and Shaw continued to press her to accept an actor of her own level.

'O Stella, Stellarum [he wrote on the green writing paper which he invariably used when he had a headache], 'there is nothing more certain in the process of the suns than that if you attempt management on the single star system, nothing— not even my genius added to your own—can save you from final defeat. Male and female created He them. Your public is more than half feminine; *you* cannot satisfy their longing for a male to idealize, and how can they idealize a poor salaried employee pushed into a corner and played off the stage? Do you want to be a Duse? A hammer without an anvil? A Sandow playing with paper dumb-bells? Produce *Pygmalion* with a twenty pounds Higgins and you will have an uproarious success, but the house will be under £200. At the end of 15 or 16 weeks, the business will stagger. You will be terrified, and will spend wildly on advertisements. You will drop to £120. Alexander will smile . . . You will take *Pygmalion* off and draw away from me. Its successor will fail, because nobody will be able to endure you in anything worse than Eliza; and the very few authors who could give you anything as good, will note my fate, and go to Frohman or Alexander instead. You will struggle on until

you have lost every farthing; and then it will be
America with all its horrors to recoup yourself,
and the provinces, or retirement, for the rest of
your life, like Mrs Kendal . . .

Now having told you all this, I grow reckless
and will tell you still more terrible things.
Loraine is indispensable. I can make the cat play
Liza. It wouldn't be *my* Liza because it wouldn't
be *your* Liza. But it would be a commercially
possible Eliza. And I can't make the dog play
Higgins. That is a thing that often happens: it is
not the best part that is the difficulty. And apart
from the part, where am I to find a man to stand
up to you on the stage? . . .

Who, then, is to be your complement? the John
Drew to your Ada Rehan, the Irving to your
Ellen Terry? I must have a heroic Higgins. And
I must not ruin you. Nor myself. I could not love
thee, dear, so much, loved I not money more.
Name your man. . . .

Edmund Gwenn and Hilda Trevelyan sent
today to offer the Vaudeville on any terms you
like under their management. . . .

at your feet, G.B.S.

Mrs Pat's reply was evasive and arrived punc-
tually the next day.

I haven't had a minute to answer your funny
green pages—I wish you weren't so early Victorian—I see your point of view clearly.

You must let Loraine have the play if Higgins

33

is more important than Eliza. But he and I cannot be forced into a partnership—that would
never do.

One knows only too well that a 'two star' show
is better than a 'one star' and that an 'all-star'
show is fit only for Kings and Queens!!

The two star affairs you quote were more or less
bound by cupid! . . .

Before making up your mind, you would
naturally like to know what theatre and the
financial strength of the undertaking: this, of
course, will be put before you, and you will be
discreet—I shall know in a very few days.

I would be very unhappy if I couldn't feel the
very best had been done for your brilliant play—
I would far rather lose 'Eliza'.

My love to you and to your Charlotte too.

Beatrice Stella.

10 Adelphi Terrace, W.C.
5th July 1912.

I don't want anything put before me. I am an
artist and don't understand finance. I want my
Liza and I want my Higgins. If you are unkind
about them I shall sit down and cry until I get
them. I won't choose between them. I must have
my Liza and no other Liza. There is no other
Liza and there can be no other Liza. I wrote the
play to have my Liza. And I must have a proper
Higgins for my Liza. I won't listen to reason: I
will sit there and howl. I can howl for twenty

34

years, getting louder and louder all the time . . .
I won't be offered the Best and then refused poor
Bobby, who *is* the best. I will have a better if you
can find him, because nobody is good enough for
my Liza . . . I don't want to force anybody into
anything. I only want to see my play with my
Liza properly supported in it; and until I get that
I want to do nothing but yell. If you had a heart
you would not be so obstinate and unreasonable.
All I ask is to have my own way in everything,
and to see my Liza as often as possible.

I have gone through my card index and could
name you twenty far better Higgins than any
you have thought of; but they are none of them
good enough; I'd rather die than see you dragged
down to second class by them: I'd as soon ask you
to wear a contract dress at £3. 4s. 2d. If you won't
have Loraine then we must wait until somebody
else whom you *will* have comes to the front and
proves his mettle. And I shall cry, cry, cry all the
time, and there will be a great wave of public
feeling against you for your cruelty. And I will
write such a play for Lena Ashwell, my dear Lena
who really loves me. So there! G.B.S.

                    33 Kensington Square.
Oh darling what a letter!
I call you 'darling' because 'dear Mr Shaw'
means nothing at all—whilst darling means most
dear and most dear means a man, and a mind and
a speaking—such as you and your mind and

your speech. Now please pull yourself together and tell me whether I may get on with business or no. I too have London and provincial rights and I would like permission to play Eliza after Loraine and Cissy Loftus have finished with it in New York—If you say 'No', 'No', 'No'—then add 'but you may come and see me whenever you like and Charlotte too—we are friends.'

I long to get on with the whole thing and call rehearsals on September 1st or else get off—you know how *much* I want to work with you—and as sure as one can feel—I feel sure (Shaw)—There's a nice original joke—. Beatrice Stella.

Theatrical politics being what they are, the most elaborate plans of actors and authors can be destroyed overnight. Luckily for Mrs Pat, neither Loraine, nor Cissy Loftus ever played *Pygmalion* in New York, or in England or, indeed, anywhere; so the English and American fields were left wide open for her pleasure.

★

Casting problems and theatrical politics apart, there was a far more serious reason for the delay. On July 12th, a week after she had written the above letter to Shaw, she was involved in a serious street accident. The taxi which was taking her to the theatre one evening collided with another in a road near the Albert Hall. Her head smashed through one of the windows, missing haemorrhage of the brain

36

and a speedy death by a fraction of an inch. Screaming hysterically, her face streaming with blood, she was taken to St George's Hospital, treated for bruises, contusions and cuts, bandaged, sedated and finally allowed to return home. 'She was not badly hurt,' said the press with its usual misinformed optimism, 'she will be back at the St James's Theatre to resume her part in *Bella Donna* to-morrow.' The press was wrong on both points: she *was* badly hurt and the damage was serious enough to keep her away from the theatre for a fortnight. In great agony she nursed two black eyes and a swollen jaw, suffering a series of blinding headaches, terrified that she might be disfigured for life, and wondering if she would ever be able to act again.

Without her, *Bella Donna* had no attraction for the public, and, after struggling unhappily with rapidly diminishing houses, Alexander finally surrendered to the inevitable and withdrew it at the beginning of August. The following week she was declared well enough to travel. Sir Edward and Lady Stracey, two long-standing friends, took her in their Rolls Royce to Aix-les-Bains to rest, to relax in the sunshine, and to take a course of healing baths. These, unhappily, had an adverse effect on her health, and on her return to London, her doctor, Sir Alfred Fripp, ordered her to bed where she remained for six months. It was a very difficult period for everybody; there were her good days when she was well and cheerful and could receive visitors and laugh and chatter and make excited plans about her return to the theatre, and there were her bad days when the headaches returned, the slightest noise upset her, and she was forced to lie in darkness and silence. Fortunately, she was well cared for with Beo and his American wife, Helen, and young Stella, all in devoted attendance. Celebrities from every walk of life came to Kensington Square to pay her sympathetic homage including Sarah Bernhardt, a vision of moleskin and sable who struggled up six flights of stairs supported by Beo, with exhausted cries of 'Oh, Mon Dieu! Mon Dieu! Vertige, quelle vertige!'

But in the end it was Shaw who made life tolerable for her: through his intelligent and perceptive grasp of medicine and human psychology, he understood not only the extent but also the nature of her illness. The stupid infatuation of the previous summer was a thing of the past: what he now offered her was infinitely more valuable—a generous, unselfish and loving friendship, the only sort which matters. At a time when he was exceptionally busy with rehearsals for three plays simultaneously and the endless cross-country journeys which they involved, he still found time to call on her several times a week when he talked and joked and sang and laughed, revelling in the mischievous fun and the smile he brought to her face. He wrote her endless letters full of lovers' nonsense, poems, stories, gossip; he sent her books and papers and gave her another reading of *Pygmalion*, this time from galley proofs specially set up by a printer in Edinburgh. Finally, he showed his true understanding of the practicalities of her situation by giving her money. This was something she urgently needed and he appears to have been the only one of her friends who realized it. She had never had any money of her own, and now that she could not work she was in great financial distress. Shaw gave her a thousand pounds to pay her doctors' and nurses' fees, her convalescence expenses and her debts. It was a gesture she never forgot.

By the summer of 1913 she was better, but although the physical recovery was complete, with her beauty restored undiminished and no outward sign that it had ever been damaged, the psychological effects of the accident were deeper and more far-reaching than anybody, even Shaw, realized. The system had received a profound shock and the damage to her nerves had had a disastrous effect on her judgement and her temper. It can truthfully be said that she never completely recovered from the accident for her most outrageous behaviour dated from this time. She had always been difficult but now she became impossible, and it was then that the deplorable conduct started which eventually led to what was a virtual banishment from the West End theatre.

In June, she was well enough to resume the infinitely futile casting discussions over *Pygmalion*. Just about every leading actor in London was considered but all, for one reason or another, were found to be unacceptable. 'Gerald du Maurier?' suggested Shaw, and this was a clever move, for Mrs Pat had worked with him several times on tour and was very fond of him. 'Darling Gerald,' she smiled, 'but no, I think not. He's too young and—bless him—far too ugly; I could never act with a face like that!' Shaw suggested Lewis Waller, whose good looks, silver trumpet voice and virility had made him an object of hysterical adulation from young women who had formed what was, in fact, the first fan club in theatrical history—the Keen On Waller Society or K.O.W.S., known cynically to their elders as the Sacred Kows. Mrs Pat had a warm professional regard for Waller's acting ability, which was considerable, but she did not wish to act with him. 'He's far too handsome,' she said firmly, 'it would never do.' H. B. Irving was put forward and would have made a very good Higgins but Mrs Pat found him pompous and lacking in humour, two unforgivable sins in her eyes. Matheson Lang was too fat and physically repulsive and as for C. Aubrey Smith, 'Really, Joey,' she exclaimed in exasperation, 'What nonsense. I could never act with a cricket bat!'

Discussions were resumed with Alexander but he had other plans and was only interested in *Pygmalion* as a possible stopgap till the autumn, which Shaw refused. Instead, Alexander presented yet another revival of *The Second Mrs Tanqueray*, and since she needed the money and had been inactive quite long enough, Mrs Pat consented to return to the St James's and resume her old part of Paula, which kept her busy and solvent till Christmas.

In the meantime, while the English theatre

managers were shilly-shallying, the foreign theatre managers stepped in, smartly and decisively. For a long time, Continental impresarios had been dismayed and frustrated by the fact that they had been allowed to present Shaw's plays only after they had already been butchered by the English press, whose charming habit it had always been to inform the world that Shaw's plays were dull, blasphemous, unpopular and financially unsuccessful. From this there rose an urgent demand from the German theatre directors that they should be allowed to produce them first. Shaw, who had no particular loyalties to one country above another, consented readily; and to the rage and mortification of the English theatrical establishment, his subsequent plays, with only a few unimportant exceptions, invariably had their first performances abroad. *Pygmalion* therefore had its world première in Vienna in October 1913, Liza being played by Frau Tilla Durieux, one of the Hofburgtheater's comedy stars. This was quickly followed by further productions at the Lessing Theatre, Berlin, and the Royal Dramatic Theatre, Stockholm, with Mme Harriet Boise as Eliza. Owing to a printer's error and the Swedish habit of translating even the names of the characters, the heroine of the play was listed in the programme as Miss Eliza *Littledoo*.

The London press was, a trifle illogically, roused to considerable fury by what they called disloyalty, and the theatre-owners were heard to mutter against Shaw, more in sorrow than in anger, considering that he had been rather underhand about it all, and that his conduct had not been that of a gentleman. But it did have one fortunate effect: it roused them to action. Before then, the very existence of *Pygmalion* had been known only to a privileged few; but with the applause of the Continental press echoing throughout Europe, everybody knew about it. Then, as now, there was nothing like a resounding success abroad to arouse the interest of the West End overlords, and even the great actor-managers themselves were not above a little discreet scheming and lobbying, anxious—as Leaders of The Profession—to secure the rights of the play, Alexander having passed round the word that it was a winner. Like medieval knights in a tournament, the theatrical knights of the West End started to pursue this Fair Lady. They were eventually joined in the hunt by the actor-manager of the magnificent and beautiful His Majesty's Theatre, that fine old English gentleman with the Dutch-Jewish father, staring eyes, a peculiar foreign-sounding voice, and one of the oddest personalities of the Edwardian theatre—Sir Herbert Beerbohm Tree.

3

SHAW AND TREE HAD KNOWN EACH
other for over twenty years, since Shaw's reign of
terror as the dramatic critic of *The Saturday Review*
and Tree's regime as actor-manager over the road at
the Theatre Royal, Haymarket. They had been
friendly, though casual acquaintances; if they
appeared to have little in common, they found, in
fact, much to like and admire in each other. Tree
liked Shaw's mischievous, arrogant insolence, and
Shaw was delighted by a certain grotesque fantasy
element in Tree's character and personality. By the
time *Pygmalion* entered into Tree's life, he had
developed into a typical, dreamy, witty eccentric
Englishman. He was blessed with an unusually lov-
able nature and was quite incapable of harbouring
grudges or resentfully taking criticisms of his acting
as personal insults. This last was a quality he sorely
needed, for when Shaw launched his assault course
on the West End Theatre, he attacked Tree even
more fiercely than the others. 'The only way Mr
Tree can play Falstaff,' Shaw once said, 'is to get himself born all over again and as differently as possible.'
Tree laughed heartily, agreed with every word, and
continued to play Falstaff exactly as before.

While Shaw might laugh at Tree and his elaborate
productions, he realized that Tree was at least
attempting to find plays of literary quality. Hesketh
Pearson, in his excellent biography of Tree, states

that in addition to Shakespeare he put on plays by Maeterlinck, Brieux and Wilde and he appreciated the genius of Ibsen at a time when the other actors and nearly all the critics were describing his work as a sort of intellectual sewer. Tree was, in fact, the first West End manager to put on an Ibsen play, *An Enemy of the People*, which was presented for a series of matinées in the 'nineties.

He had married a school-teacher and amateur actress, Maud Holt, a lady of considerable charm but limited acting ability. Tree sensibly refused to give her leading parts at His Majesty's in startling contrast to the other leading actors of the period, who shamelessly starred their not-very-talented wives opposite them; the great actor-managers' wives were the price the public had to pay for the great actor-managers. It was difficult to reconcile the frustrations of being an occasional actress with the responsibilities of being Lady Tree, but Maud managed it with dignity. Tree adored her but was unable to be faithful to her. She loved him very much, accepted his philanderings gracefully, and gave him three daughters, Viola, Iris and Felicity.

He was one of the few amongst the West End fraternity to appreciate the theatrical genius in Shaw's plays when everybody else was contemptuously dismissing them as unactable, and he had already made several attempts to produce a Shaw play at His Majesty's. He attempted to persuade Shaw to write a play about Don Quixote, a project which came to nothing; but in 1909 Shaw wrote a matinée. Tree, who had just been knighted and was very conscious of his newfound dignity, objected to the blasphemous language in the scene where Blanco swears at God. So did the Lord Chamberlain, who refused it a licence unless the offending passage was omitted. Shaw bluntly refused, the play was cancelled and was not produced till long after the war. This was the Edwardian public's loss for they were deprived not only of one of Shaw's most original plays, but also of the unprecedented and unimaginable spectacle of Sir Herbert Beerbohm Tree dressed as a cowboy.

In the five years which had passed, he continued to hanker after a Shaw play, and then came the first whispers of *Pygmalion*. Like all the others he had heard about it from Alexander, but now an entirely unexpected stumbling block presented itself. It seemed that if Alexander did not wish to act with Mrs Pat, she, in her turn, did not wish to act with Tree. When Shaw first mentioned his name as a possible Higgins, she angrily refused to listen. 'He treated me so abominably during my last engagement in his theatre, that his name must on no account be mentioned in my presence. Never again!' Shaw was very intrigued by this surprising statement, for Mrs Pat had played three engagements at His Majesty's with every outward sign of harmony and satisfaction. What could have gone wrong? He made inquiries about this supposedly unpardonable behaviour and he found, as he suspected, that it was nothing, only a storm in a teacup. But although Tree's behaviour had not been unpardonable, it had certainly been a little strange.

It appeared that in 1909 just after the abortive *Blanco Posnet* affair, Tree had presented a play, *Beethoven* a heavy-handed poetical drama of quite inconceivable badness translated from the French by Louis Parker, in which Tree, superbly made up and with sets and furniture cunningly enlarged and cheated to make him look small, scored a huge personal success as Beethoven. Its duration was a little over two hours, and since Edwardian theatregoers liked their money's worth in quantity as well as quality, he arranged for the evening to be rounded off with a one-act afterpiece, a turgid Russian drama called *Expiation* in which Mrs Pat played the leading part of Olga, a spy who sacrifices her life to save her husband. The play was so bad that even she was not able to save it from being barracked by the public and torn to pieces by the press. This was, after all, one of the occupational hazards of the Profession and she could take it in her stride, but what she did object to was Tree's extraordinary behaviour during the mercifully brief run of the play.

On the first night, Tree played *Beethoven* to a full house, but when she made her entrance as Olga, the spy in *Expiation*, Mrs Pat was very surprised and perturbed to discover that the theatre was half empty. This happened every night with alarming regularity: full houses for *Beethoven*, rows of empty seats for *Expiation*. One evening she decided to investigate the matter. The loudspeaker system had not yet been invented: it was necessary to go on to the stage to hear what people were saying. One night she stood in the wings and she heard with mounting anger the curtain speech which Tree made at the end of *Beethoven*. It was the routine speech which all actor-managers used to make to their audiences and this in itself was not remarkable, but in this case the timing and omissions left much to be desired. 'Ladies and gentlemen,' he said, 'thank you so very much for your splendid reception of our little play tonight. I am deeply *honoured*, so very *touched*, so *happy* . . . may I end by wishing you a safe journey home . . . and God bless you all.' Without actually saying so, the speech was so subtly dismissive, that he contrived to give the audience the impression that the evening was over, whereupon those members of the audience who had not bothered to read their programme carefully, rose and left the theatre. Shaw was boundlessly delighted when he heard about it and attempted to argue and coax the fuming Mrs Pat into a more tolerant frame of mind.

'Come on now, Stella,' he chuckled, 'it was only his absent-mindedness, you know what he was like.

'It was outrageous,' she cried.

'He'd probably forgotten all about your play himself.'

'Forgotten! Me?'

'It wasn't a very good play, was it now?'

'That was *not* the point.'

'You had a dreadful time in it, Stella,' he said firmly, 'and you were quite dreadful having it!' But

Mrs Pat refused to discuss the matter. Tree was most definitely not to be considered.

This was a deadlock. Shaw had little interest in his plays once he had finished writing them, so he washed his hands of the whole business and took no further trouble, and *Pygmalion* might have remained on the shelf indefinitely and never been produced at all, were it not for a happy stroke of fate, good luck cleverly disguised as bad. It was now January 1914 and the revival of *The Second Mrs Tanqueray* was withdrawn. Once again Mrs Pat was unemployed and soon became insolvent. She had always been wasteful, extravagant, absurdly generous and quite incapable of living within her income, however large it might be. 'How *glorious* to have £700 one week and nothing the next,' she used to say. Her creditors who had been so patient with her during her illness, now became so pressing that she had no alternative but to go to Shaw and humbly ask him: 'Well, what about Tree?' as if the idea had been hers all along. All misunderstandings were forgiven if not forgotten, she went to Tree with a copy of the play and asked him to invite Shaw to give a reading, adding as a further inducement that she herself was available and willing to play Eliza. An appointment was made and one afternoon in late January, Shaw read the play to Tree in the Dome. This was the luxury flat which Tree had fitted out at the top of the theatre, furnished and decorated with truly medieval, monastic splendour. Also present were Mrs Pat, Henry Dana, Tree's business-manager, and a number of Tree's

Garrick Club friends.

The reading was a big success and Tree laughed and chuckled continuously throughout the play. 'Very good, Mr Shaw, very amusing,' he said at the end, 'quite delightful, most original, it's really very charming. . . . I'd like to do it . . . but there's one thing, only a small point, hardly worth mentioning but it does bother me a little. . . .'

'Well?' said Shaw.

'The language. Really, I don't think . . . I know it's very amusing but . . . not in *my* beautiful theatre . . . I can't imagine what people will say . . .'

'They'll love it,' said Shaw firmly. 'When Mrs Pat has said it, then everybody will be saying it, you'll see.'

'But it's never been heard before in the theatre.'

'Yes it has,' said Shaw. 'Macbeth, as you should know.'

'Ahhh, *Shakespeare*,' said Tree airily, 'that doesn't count. You can say anything in a classic, people never listen anyway . . .'

'*The Hooligan* and *Admiral Guinea* at the Court Theatre, both produced within the last five years.'

'The *Court*,' said Tree disdainfully, 'yes, but this is the West End. . . . No, it's a pity because it is so very amusing and striking, but I really *don't* think . . . look, if you'll cut that word I'll consider producing the play . . .'

Shaw's still red eyebrows shot up a full inch. 'Sir Herbert,' he trumpeted, 'if you cut the word I won't even consider *allowing* you to produce the play!'

'The question is not for us to decide, Chief,' It was Henry Dana speaking, Tree's long-suffering business manager. 'The play has not yet been submitted to the censor. If he forbids it, then the matter will have been decided for us. If he finds it acceptable, you will be quite safe in allowing it.'

'He's quite right,' said Shaw. 'A few people might be shocked, but the majority will love it. The world is changing rapidly. No, I don't anticipate any trouble from the censor, not after the roasting I gave him after he banned *Blanco Posnet* and if there is, I'll let loose such an avalanche of scorn he'll beg to be abolished.'

The matter rested there for a full week. Tree sent the script to the Lord Chamberlain's office and waited a little nervously for the result. To his astonishment *Pygmalion* had a speedy passage through the administrative machinery of St James's Palace and was returned within a week without any requests for changes in the text. Shaw had evidently been right. In fact, the Lord Chamberlain's decision was not as surprising as it seemed: he had, after all, approved of the Word twice before. In *The Hooligan* by W. S. Gilbert, the prisoner on his way to his execution had said to the bullying warder: 'Take your bloody hands off me.' And in *Admiral Guinea* a drunken old sailor said: 'Sink me if he ain't a-singin' like a bloody blackbird.' In neither case did the word provoke the slightest comment. Greatly encouraged, Tree engaged a company which included

Philip Merivale, Carlotta Addison, Margaret Bussé, Irene Delisse, Geraldine Olliffe and Edmund Gurney, all of whom had worked for him before, and *Pygmalion* was announced for production at His Majesty's Theatre, starting rehearsals in the middle of February.

But there was one little matter which had to be decided before rehearsals could start, and that was the question of artistic authority. Who was to direct the play? In those golden, distant days before the First World War finally destroyed the actor-manager system, the director—as we now know him—had only just begun to emerge from his anonymity. In fact, until a few years before, he could hardly be said to have existed at all. It was William Poel who put forward the heretical idea that there should ideally be somebody not involved in the play, not as author and certainly not as leading actor, who should decide on all artistic matters and with total authority over everybody. Until then, it was automatically assumed that the great actor-managers, who owned their theatres and were accustomed to acting their own leading parts, would direct the plays themselves, unless the author was sufficiently famous and also a man of the theatre, like Gilbert, Granville-Barker, Pinero, and Shaw. Under normal circumstances, Tree would have directed *Pygmalion*, but these circumstances were anything but normal, because Mrs Pat had been in management and had directed the plays she had appeared in. Shaw knew her and he knew Tree. He knew that Mrs Pat was more interested in vehicles than in plays, which she regarded merely as a tiresome but necessary background for her own performance, and directed them accordingly if she got the chance; but now she wasn't going to be given that chance. As for Tree, Shaw knew that *Pygmalion* represented a completely new departure from the accepted His Majesty's repertoire, and that the old standards of production which suited those spectacular costume dramas that had always been Tree's great joy, would not work for a play which was all clever dialogue and virtually no action.

Shaw bluntly refused to entrust his brainchild to the splendid but capricious talents of the great actor-manager, let alone those of his leading lady. He insisted on directing *Pygmalion* himself. The seeds of discontent were thus planted, preparing the way for a really magnificently explosive situation. The duet of personalities was now a trio, and the music which thundered and screamed round the Dome of the famous theatre was as dramatic and as colourful as the play which inspired it.

But this is to anticipate: at the beginning, as it usually is in the theatre, it was all sweetness and light, declarations of mutual esteem and promises of good behaviour. 'Oh goodness, we're in for it and let's be *very* clever,' wrote Mrs Pat to Shaw after the first rehearsal. 'Tree's fixed and you can manage the lot of us and then indeed you'll be a *great man*. Tree wants to be friendly and his admiration for you and the play is ENORMOUS. I'll be as tame as a mouse, and oh, *so* obedient. I wonder if you can get what you want out of me—I feel a little afraid.'

ottoman, so pleased to get rid of the visitors that he becomes almost civil. Freddy comes back from the balcony—appears at the window

CLARA. Oh yes! we have three at-homes to go to still. ~~Good-bye, Professor Higgins.~~

HIGGINS [~~shaking hands with her across the ottoman~~] Good-bye. Be sure you try on that small talk at the three at-homes. Dont be nervous about it. Pitch it in strong.

CLARA [*all smiles*] I will. Good-bye, Mrs Higgins. Good-bye, Colonel Pickering. [*Turning again to Higgins, who is accompanying her to the door*] Such nonsense, all this early Victorian prudery!

HIGGINS. Such damned nonsense!

CLARA. Such bloody nonsense!

MRS EYNSFORD HILL [*convulsively*] Clara!

CLARA. Ha! ha! [*She goes out radiant, conscious of being thoroughly up to date*].

FREDDY [*to Higgins*] Well, I ask you— [*He gives it up, and comes to Mrs Higgins, followed by Higgins, who comes to Mrs Hill*] Good-bye.

MRS HIGGINS [*shaking hands*] Good-bye. Would you like to meet Miss Doolittle again?

FREDDY. Yes, I should, most awfully.

MRS HIGGINS. Well, you know my days.

FREDDY. Yes. Thanks awfully. Good-bye. [*He goes out*].

MRS EYNSFORD HILL. Good-bye, Mr Higgins.

HIGGINS. Good-bye. Good-bye.

MRS EYNSFORD HILL [*to Pickering*] It's no use. I shall never be able to bring myself to use that word.

PICKERING. Dont. It's not compulsory, you know. Youll get on quite well without it.

MRS EYNSFORD HILL. Only, Clara is so down on me if I am not positively reeking with the latest slang. Good-bye.

PICKERING. Good-bye [*They shake hands*].

MRS EYNSFORD HILL [*to Mrs Higgins*] You mustnt mind Clara. We're so poor! and she gets so few parties, poor child! She doesnt quite know. [*Mrs Higgins, seeing that her eyes*

Drawn by Bert Thomas

PORTRAIT OF A YOUNG DRAMATIST READING EXTRACTS
FROM HIS LATEST PLAY TO NATIVE OF BILLINGSGATE

The Tatler)

4

IT IS UNLIKELY THAT SHAW WOULD
have rushed to take charge of the production if he
had known in advance just how much trouble he was
going to have with his two stars.

Since the death of Irving in 1905, it was Tree
who, as senior actor-manager and Irving's legiti-
mate successor, was generally acknowledged as the
First Gentleman of the London theatre. He was an
actor of amazing accomplishment and versatility; he
had extraordinary imagination and theatrical flair,
and the public which flocked to His Majesty's
revelled in the brilliantly studied characterization he
presented, and the splendidly colourful realism of his
productions. He inspired the most amazing love and
loyalty in his followers who would far rather see him
being bad than most other actors being good. But
those who worked with him in the theatre had a very
different story to tell. Vague, absent-minded, extravagant, irresponsible, with no knowledge of theatrical
etiquette, or sense of its discipline, it was a perpetual
amazement to outsiders that the theatre survived
and that its productions ever saw the light of day. In
any other business, Tree would have been bankrupt
inside a week; but the theatre is happily quite unlike
any other sort of business and the normal economic
rules do not apply. In the theatre, you are either making money so lavishly that extravagance and dis-
organization can't stop it, or you are losing it so

heavily that all the economy and care in the world can't save you from ruin. Tree had very few failures: he had a flair for spotting winners, and his productions usually made money. Luckily, he employed first-rate men; they knew the difficult task of stage and theatre management, they could take the boring routine work out of his hands, and he had the good sense to let them do it without interference.

The turmoil and chaos of rehearsals at His Majesty's dismayed those who were accustomed to the calm professional efficiency of the Lyceum, the St James's or Wyndhams. At His Majesty's, nobody seemed to have a clear idea what to do or who was supposed to do what. Nobody seemed to have a clearly defined function as they did in more sanely organized theatres, everybody interfered in everybody else's business. All day the theatre was filled with strangers, wandering in and out of the stalls and circles, on and off the stage. Nobody knew who they were. In fact, they were Tree's retinue, for he collected people as the Pied Piper collected children. Sometimes they were journalists, for Tree liked newspaper people, being one of the first actor-managers to go out of his way to cultivate friendly relations with the press. Sometimes they were backers or composers; sometimes playwrights, on whose plays he had an option, or unemployed actors for whom he felt an affection but had no wish to employ. Sometimes they were rival managers. Sometimes they were just casual friends whom he had met at the Garrick Club or even in the street and invited to the theatre to make themselves thoroughly at home. 'Come into my beautiful theatre and watch the rehearsals of my beautiful play and if anything strikes you, don't hesitate to speak up,' he would say. This they certainly did, interrupting his rehearsals with suggestions which were sometimes accepted, usually ignored. Hesketh Pearson, who was a member of the His Majesty's Company for some years, relates how delighted these visitors were when Tree said: 'Every dogma has his day,' and how proceedings were discontinued by the laughter which greeted, 'I shall give a banquet to my critics and on each plate I shall put copies of their articles, in order that they may eat their words.'

In the babel of discordant voices that broke out during a scene, Tree's voice could be heard asking rather sadly: 'May I be allowed a word in this theatre?' The only people who ever got things done were Henry Dana, and Stanley Bell. If Henry Dana was a long-suffering business manager, Stanley Bell was an even longer-suffering stage-manager. But until Shaw saw their names on the programme and posters under their respective titles, he could never be quite sure that they didn't belong to the Garrick Club retinue. They certainly knew how to get things done, and it is perhaps just as much due to them as to Shaw that *Pygmalion* ever had a first night.

This was the madhouse in which Shaw found himself when he called the first rehearsal on February 10th. Like all true professionals he was appalled and set to work to bring some order into the chaos. The company was called for eleven every morning and work continued with only an hour's break for lunch till five-thirty every afternoon. The rehearsals were scheduled to last for a month but they dragged on for two and they were inconceivably dreadful. It was up-hill work all the way because, quite apart from every-thing else, Tree was seldom there. He was frequently late; he spent the greater part of the day roaming around the theatre talking to visitors in his dressing-room or up in the Dome watching Shaw rehearse the other actors from the safety of the dress circle—anything rather than go onto the stage and get down to learning his lines which he always hated and was never good at, particularly when the lines were by Shaw and the author, in his most tiresome and schoolmasterish way, was there to supervise.

He really had no sense of time and the amount he contrived to waste was a perpetual thorn in Shaw's side. If Dana called on him and told him that he had a visitor, he would excuse himself from the stage, walk off and leave the rest of the company to await his return which might be minutes or even hours. Shaw would naturally continue with the understudy and eventually Tree would return and be deeply indignant that Shaw had not waited for him. For example, one day Dana appeared and told Tree that the *Times* theatre correspondent had called and begged the favour of an exclusive interview. 'Shall I ask him to return later, Chief?' he asked. Tree smiled expansively. 'Nonsense, my dear Dana,' he said, beamingly, 'I'll see him now. No Times like the present,' which elicited a delighted laugh from his attendant retinue. Tree took the *Times* man up to the Dome and was away for two hours.

'Well, here's our absentee landlord,' said Shaw sarcastically, when Tree returned. 'Good of you to come, Sir Herbert. Now are you *sure* you can spare the time?'

But Shaw's sarcasm finally had its effect and it was noticed that Tree's absences during rehearsals became less frequent and finally stopped altogether.

As time went by, and everything and everyone seemed to interfere with his production, Shaw, finding himself free to interfere, interfered not only in his own department but in every other department as well. This, of course, infuriated Tree who alone had been in command since he had built the theatre in 1897. Shaw did not appear to realize that, with the theatre to administer, there were good reasons for Tree's absence, and that if his production methods seemed careless, they did work and did produce the most amazing results. And although Tree's bad memory aroused more Shavian wrath than anything else, Hesketh Pearson has pointed out that his performance was always more spontaneous when he didn't know his lines.

Hesketh Pearson has stated that his method was to imagine himself into the part, so that he became the man with study. Seymour Hicks said that as a character actor Tree was unrivalled, stating that he had never seen a man who had so varied a range. But how could this be achieved without study and preparation? Genius in an actor cannot be described; it can only be felt. The difference between the acting of Irving and that of Tree was the difference between hypnotism and enchantment. But enchantment and intuition were the last things which Shaw wanted; what he demanded of his actors was a clear propounding of his argument without tricks, and the complete veneration of his script down to the last comma.

Tree and Mrs Pat had much in common and there are some striking parallels in their careers. The sad truth was that, for all their amazing gifts, they rose to their position of stardom with something less than a star's complete equipment. The great actors whom Shaw had seen in his youth—Charles Kean, Phelps, Fechter, Macready, Barry Sullivan, Irving—had all endured many years of struggle in poverty and obscurity. They had come up the hard way and in those days it was very hard indeed; they were all supremely dedicated men who took themselves and their profession very seriously. Tree's attitude to his profession was essentially mischievous and light-hearted, whereas Mrs Pat had started because she urgently needed money to support her two children in her husband's absence. In both cases they had enjoyed a sensational rise to overnight fame after an exceptionally short apprenticeship of little over five years, and in both cases success had come too quickly and too easily for them to acquire more than a superficial command of acting technique.

They were well aware of how to take advantage of their personalities, which were astonishing and unique: both had an instinctive command of theatrical effect, though having achieved something striking *once*, they could never repeat it without spoiling it, the mark of the inspired amateur which indeed is what they both were. They knew what effect they wanted without knowing how to get it: they knew the climax of their art, but not the start. For example, Mrs Pat did not know how to use the front of the stage; she was nervous of the footlights and Shaw had to show her. Also, she insisted on having too much limelight on her face: she did not realize that this blotted out all the character and cast unflattering shadows everywhere, so that it looked, not like the beautifully sculptured head it really was, but like a dinner plate with two prunes on it. It is unlikely if theatrical history has ever produced two people who were so professional in their skill and so amateurish in their attitude.

It was ironic that it was they who regarded Shaw as the amateur, an outsider who knew nothing whatever about the theatre. They treated him with such charming condescension that Shaw could not forbear to comment on it. 'Have you noticed something?' he once said to them. 'Here are we three, no longer young who have all risen to the heights of our profession and have enjoyed great success—yet we're treating each other like beginners who have to be taught everything!'

But there were other sources of tension which went much deeper than a mere matter of unpunctuality and rehearsal etiquette. Tree rather fancied himself as an author and had actually published a volume of essays called *Thoughts and Afterthoughts*. The literary talent on display therein was not remarkable, though Shaw, when commenting on their style and polish, had some kind things to say. But in fact Tree was a frustrated playwright, and though he did not have the creative talent and powers of concentration to write a play of his own, he made up for this by compulsively re-writing everybody else's. Where the author was dead, living abroad, or otherwise inaccessible, he was able to do this with impunity—in fact, it must be admitted that the great success of *Trilby* was largely due to his efforts in this direction. The plays did not always benefit from this treatment, but his own parts were always splendidly extended and improved.

But with Shaw, it was a very different matter. The irresistible force now met the immovable object with the inevitable result: Shaw would not budge an inch nor yield to his suggestions in the slightest degree. Tree wasted a lot of time by trying to re-write *Pygmalion* in a laudable effort to bring it up to the His Majesty's standard. His intentions were always amiable and sincere. He really wanted to do his best for the play, regarding it as his sacred duty to make it into an effective piece of stage entertainment. It never once occurred to him that Shaw had already done this. In fact, he never understood that Shaw was a supreme master of his difficult art and had in *Pygmalion* produced a play which was, down to the last detail, a completely workable dramatic creation; he could never grasp that all he was required to do was to fit himself into the picture as best as he could, like a piece in a jigsaw puzzle. It was all very bewildering for him and he wasted a lot of time in futile attempts to persuade Shaw to make changes and additions. Anticipating *My Fair Lady* by nearly half a century, he even suggested a ball-scene; 'a beautiful ball-scene for my beautiful theatre, Shaw, you certainly missed a heaven-sent opportunity there,' he said.

'No,' said Shaw firmly, but Tree was not easily deterred; he continued as if Shaw had not spoken. 'I can just see it, a street scene, Park Lane, the Embassy all lit up with an awning, dozens of taxis and cars drawing up and . . .'

'The London County Council will only allow us one taxi,' said Shaw, 'have you forgotten that?'

'. . . and then a transformation scene,' continued Tree smiling happily. 'We are in the ball-room, foot-men in livery, chandeliers, a real orchestra playing a waltz, hundreds of supers in gorgeous clothes, Eliza comes in with Pickering, she is wearing a beautiful gown with jewels . . .'

'No!' repeated Shaw firmly, 'it's not necessary,' but he might as well have saved his breath for Tree was not listening; he was speaking like a prophet in-spired. 'Then there will be a huge curved staircase and then . . . then . . . then *I* shall come on at the top of the staircase . . . I shall wear a purple-lined cloak over my dress-suit, I shall descend the staircase and then I shall present Eliza to the Ambassador, perhaps he will be Turkish with a gold and black uniform and a fez, and then I will waltz with Eliza all over the stage and . . .'

'Sir Herbert!' interrupted Shaw, speaking now very slowly and carefully as if to an idiot child, which in a sense he was, 'why do you always want to gild the lily? If I thought the ball-scene such as you have described was dramatically necessary, believe me, I would have written one. You calmly propose to spend hundreds of pounds on an elaborate set, costumes and effects to produce a scene which—if I know you—will last as long as the rest of the play put together, and for what? Simply to make a point which I have made very simply and effectively in a single page of dialogue in Act Four.' 'Aah!' interrupted Tree eagerly, 'but don't you see, if you do as I suggest, we can cut your Act Four'. 'No!' roared Shaw. 'If this was a musical comedy at the Gaiety, it would be a different matter, but it isn't.'

Shaw's refusal was a source of complete bewilderment to Tree who continued to pester him for opportunities to create those spectacular scenes which he and his audiences loved. 'We have mistaken our professions, Sir Herbert,' said Shaw irritably one day, 'you should have been the author and I the actor.' Tree was highly flattered by this. 'Oh, do you *really* think so?' he said, beaming delightedly, 'how very, *very* kind.'

Exasperation with his leading man's persistence on this point and others, finally provoked Shaw to action. Having arranged all the preliminary stage business and given some shape and order to the production, he took Tree aside and told him 'quite cordially to put on the play through in his own way and shook the dust of the theatre from my feet! This happened twice. On both occasions I had to yield to urgent appeals from other members of the cast to return; on both occasions Tree took leave of me as if it had been very kind of me to look in as I was passing to see his rehearsals, and received me on my return as if it were still more friendly of me to come back and see how he was getting on. I tried once or twice to believe that he was only pulling my leg: but that was incredible. His sincerity and insensibility were only too obvious. Finally, I had to fight my way through to a sort of production in the face of an unresisting, amusing, friendly, but heart-breakingly obstructive principal.'

On the stage Tree was so completely absorbed in himself and his part that he was quite unaware of the other actors on the stage, or of what they were doing or going to do; it was partly a natural vagueness, partly an intense concentration on the work in hand. This had one interesting side effect: he always seemed to have heard the lines of the other actors for the first time and even to be a little taken aback by them. There was an incident connected with this which Shaw was to remember vividly. In Act Four, there is a scene where Eliza, in a fit of ungovernable rage, throws Higgins's slippers at him. 'When we rehearsed this for the first time,' Shaw wrote shortly after Tree's death, 'I had taken care to have a very soft pair of velvet slippers provided, for I knew that Mrs Patrick Campbell was very dexterous, very strong and a dead shot. And sure enough, when we reached this passage, Tree got the slippers well and truly delivered with unerring aim bang in his face.' Shaw, warming to his theme, described the sequel in his usual highly amusing and exaggerated style: 'The effect was appalling: he had totally forgotten that there was any such incident in the play; and it seemed to him that Mrs Campbell, suddenly giving way to an impulse of diabolical wrath and hatred, had committed an unprovoked and brutal assault on him. The physical impact was nothing but the wound to his feelings was terrible. He collapsed in tears on the nearest chair and left me staring in amazement, whilst the entire personnel of the theatre crowded solicitously around him, explaining that the incident was part of the play and even exhibiting the prompt book to prove their words. But his morale was so shattered that it took a good deal of rallying and coaxing from Mrs Campbell, before he was in a condition to resume the rehearsal.'

It is possible that this was one of Tree's impish jokes, calculated to provoke Shaw; but if not, Tree had obviously made the most of his famous absent-mindedness, and Shaw, that most delightful of letter-writers, was determined to extract the last ounce of fun from the incident. He seems to have been so taken by his own version of the story that he persuaded himself that it would happen again and that Tree would be just as hurt and astonished

but dramatic incident completely lost its effect in the performance.

The battles in rehearsal continued to be appalling. Tree, with his strange mixture of sympathy and thoughtlessness, said and did the most dreadful

(*The Sketch*)

things without the least idea that they might upset people. He continued to be his maddening self. One day he would astonish and delight his staff by some totally unexpected gesture of sweetness and friendliness as when he took his call-boy or a group of small-part actors out to lunch, or invited an opinion of some piece of acting from the wardrobe mistress or stage-hands. The next day he would commit some really dreadful breach of etiquette by completely ignoring his staff's functions and privileges, as when he would ask Henry Dana to move a piece of furniture, or send Stanley Bell out to a nearby café for a glass of milk and a sandwich. This was typical of Tree. This sort of democracy was all very well but it was felt that he was the Chief and he should know his own place in the theatre even if he didn't know anybody else's. Shaw soon gave up all hope of being treated in any way except as a good friend who'd just dropped in for a chat. 'Hallo, Shaw,' Tree used to shout with enormous enthusiasm when the morning rehearsal began, 'how good to see you again. How are you? Anything I can do for you?' Since all Tree's friends were free to interfere with the production, Shaw decided to take full advantage of this liberty and interfered with everybody's department as well as his own. He gave instructions to the scene-painter, the wig-maker, the costume-designer, the programme-printer and the orchestra conductor, to such an extent, that Tree was moved to make what was for him a mildly sarcastic comment.

'I seem to have heard or read somewhere, Shaw, that plays have actually been presented in this theatre and performances actually given under its present management before you arrived on the scene. According to you this couldn't have happened. How do you account for it? With all possible respect, may I ask for your explanation?' he said grandly.

'I can't account for it, Sir Herbert,' said Shaw in desperation. 'I suppose you put a notice in the papers advertising the play and announcing that the per-

'I can't account for it, Sir Herbert,' said Shaw in desperation, 'I suppose you put a notice in the papers advertising the play and announcing that the performance will take place at eight-thirty in the evening, and then you take the money at the doors. You then have to do a play *somehow*! There is no other way of accounting for it as far as I can see.'

When Tree tried to rearrange Mrs Pat, Merivale and Gurney on the stage, giving himself a prominent position in the front, Shaw was very rude to him. 'No, Sir Herbert, it really won't do,' he shouted, 'it really won't do at all. Why don't you allow others a little bit of limelight which you have been enjoying for the last thirty years? There are other people on the stage with you, or have you forgotten that?' This was rather unfair, for Tree was well known to be a very unselfish actor and it was insults like that which were calculated to break down his imperturbable good nature, and to provoke one of his rare outbursts of bad temper. 'I've stood your insults long enough, Shaw, quite long enough. And I'll tell you something —I'm not going to *stand* for it any longer.'

'Then you'd better *sit* down,' said Shaw. Tree looked him up and down sardonically. 'A poor joke, but for once, I suppose, your own,' he riposted with a chuckle. But Shaw knew when he had gone too far: he apologized and proceeded to turn on the full extent of his Irish charm, which was irresistible to those who had never experienced it. 'No, don't lose your temper. Sir Herbert, don't lose your temper. If you could forget for a moment that you are Sir Herbert

Beerbohm Tree, actor-manager of His Majesty's and the unquestioned leader of the English theatre, and step into the part of Professor Higgins, then we'd get along together splendidly.'

Hesketh Pearson says that during the author's temporary absence from rehearsals, he was in the habit of writing highly critical letters to Tree on his handling of the part of Higgins. Mrs Pat admired Tree's patience but the truth of the matter was that most of the trouble was due to her.

Different actors required different treatment. Directors like Harley Granville-Barker used the velvet glove, limitless courtesy and a soft-voiced charm to persuade his actors to do what he wanted. But these methods were useless at His Majesty's during the rehearsals for *Pygmalion*. 'I could never bring myself to hit him hard enough,' Shaw once said, 'but as far as Mrs Pat was concerned, no poker was thick enough nor heavy enough to leave a solitary bruise on her.'

Mrs Pat's behaviour at rehearsals was, in a different way, as bad as Tree's. She was always late and nothing anybody could say or do could persuade her to be punctual. If Tree was not at the theatre, she would refuse to rehearse. 'Absolutely no point, sheer waste of time!' she would say; she would go and wait in her dressing-room until his arrival and Shaw would have to use her understudy as well as Tree's. If she did not feel like turning up, she would stay away without a word of apology or explanation. Then there was the business of the flower-basket. An item like this is not normally used in the early rehearsals since actors are too busy holding their scripts and stumbling over the furniture. Stanley Bell had ordered a flower-basket from Nathans and it was due to arrive at the end of the first week. This was not good enough for Mrs Pat; she wanted her flower-basket on the first day and she made an angry scene when Shaw told her it was not there. 'I'm a professional actress,' she said loftily, 'I'm accustomed to having my props from the beginning: that's how I know how to use them. I'm not accustomed to working with *amateurs*!' and off she sailed back to her dressing-room. Stanley Bell had to send Alfred Bellew, his assistant, to beg the loan of a basket from the flower-girls in the Opera Arcade next to the theatre. She would interrupt Shaw's directions, argue, make futile objections, question his instruction on every point, and generally make such a nuisance of herself that both Shaw and Tree would turn and order her out of the theatre. Sometimes they would turn on each other and all three of them would storm their separate ways out of the theatre, shaking the dust off their feet for ever— or so they loudly swore. But every morning at eleven o'clock, smiling, cheerful and friendly, they would reappear and continue the rehearsal as if nothing had happened. Mrs Pat started to object to Shaw's arrangement of the furniture and could be seen furtively pushing it upstage when he wasn't looking. Shaw would return it to its original place whereupon Mrs Pat would firmly push it upstage again. 'If you weren't such an amateur, Mr Shaw, you'd realize

71

that I can't play this scene with Sir Herbert and Mr Gurney looking over my shoulder,' she snapped irritably. 'You won't have to,' he replied patiently, 'I'm bringing them both downstage level with you,' but she refused to listen. Shaw went to Stanley Bell and spoke to him, quietly, but in Mrs Pat's hearing. 'Now about this furniture, Mr Bell,' he said, 'I think you'd better screw it all down . . . but I've given Mrs Campbell my full permission to do just what she pleases with the grand piano.' Mrs Pat had a piano in her dressing-room and sometimes when things became too much for her, she would rush from the stage, lock herself in her dressing-room and play her piano loudly and angrily. As always, her playing was superb, and never better than when she was in a bad temper. The company would crowd round the door to listen, and boredom and frustration would turn to enchantment as the theatre was filled with the romantic turbulent strains of Chopin, César Franck and Chaminade.

And there were days when everything went wrong: her costumes were a mess, her wigs would not fit ('I look like Caligula's grandmother!' was one of her favourite sayings on these occasions), she could not remember her lines, and the other actors—she was convinced—were trying to upstage her and spoil her performance. Then she would rage and scream like a caged tigress reducing the company and the stage staff to desperation and sometimes to tears. On one such occasion, Philip Merivale found a stage hand muttering angrily in the corner of the stage. 'I'll tell you who's a lucky bloke,' he snarled, '*Mister* Patrick Campbell.' Merivale stroked his moustache and considered the matter. 'Aaah, yes, I see what you mean; she's a very beautiful woman.' 'That's not what I mean, sir,' said the stage-hand, 'that's not why he's lucky.' Merivale looked curiously at him. 'Then why is he lucky?' The stage hand spat on the ground. 'Because he's dead. He had the good sense to get himself killed in the Boer War.'

Mrs Pat was having a lot of trouble with Eliza. Firstly, she had never played comedy before. Secondly, she was about thirty years too old for the part: this didn't matter nearly so much then as it would today, for the Edwardian audiences were quite accustomed to seeing their idols playing parts for which they were obviously too old and they didn't mind, preferring good acting and the magic appeal of a star personality, to a little matter of convincing realism . . . a public which could accept and applaud an elderly French actress playing Hamlet would accept anything. Thirdly, and this did matter much more, Eliza Doolittle was somebody completely outside her experience and knowledge of life, for what did she know or care about flower-girls? However, she did start keeping a watchful eye open for the habits and behaviour of the lower orders whenever she came into contact with them. One day she was lunching with some friends and she observed the parlour-maid who served them. 'Gracious heavens,' she laughed, and not, alas, out of the girl's hearing, 'that's just the stumpy, rickety little walk I want for

Eliza!' Also, she was having trouble with the accent which began to cause her a lot of anxiety. After a week's rehearsal, she began to wonder despairingly if she would ever get it. Others shared these doubts. 'Mrs Patrick Campbell as a cockney seems almost unimaginable,' commented the *Daily Telegraph* acidly, 'our curiosity is boundless!' Try as she may, she could not achieve the authentic rhythm of cockney without falling into the cheaply adenoidal effects so popular in the music-halls. Under Shaw's instructions she went to Covent Garden early in the morning, talked to the flower-girls, listened to them, watched them, buying many unwanted flowers in the process. No doubt she learned something, but it was Shaw's limitless patience in coaching her and his writing out her part in phonetics for private study which finally reduced those exquisite vowel sounds to the necessary degree of coarseness. Higgins teaching Eliza to speak well was neither so dedicated nor so skilled as Shaw teaching Mrs Pat to speak badly.

It was the same with her personality, for there was something about her natural Italian grace, her figure and her movement which annoyed him, and he used every trick at his fingertips to make her awkward and clumsy. 'I'm going to break you down, Stella,' he prophesied darkly, 'I'm going to make you forget that your grandfather was ever an Italian nobleman. Just remember that he had a circus and that your grandmother rode a horse in it!' A letter written in the second week of rehearsals indicates how painful this breaking-down process was for her.

My thoughts were distracted by the memory of
your misery at our work today. It needs a giant's
strength and great calmness but you will pull us
through with success I *know*. I will help you all
I can for I realize what you want, and I will give
you a simple sincere and human girl . . .
Could you come tomorrow afternoon late? I could
give you dinner and we could go through my part
together—that would help me enormously . . .
It's splendid of Tree to accept with gentle in-
difference letters which would have made a
Frenchman 'call you out'—why did he? Because
none of us can spare the time to take that side of you
that *hurts* seriously. I've learned my lesson. Stella.

Tree was also having trouble with Higgins though
his problem was the opposite of Mrs Pat's; far from
being compelled to acquire a new personality, he had
to leave his own untouched. He was a fine example
of a certain type of actor—the one who delights his
audiences but is the despair of his authors; the
brilliantly accomplished character actor who is never
happier nor more effective than when completely
transforming his own appearance and personality, but
is strangely dull when he is required simply to be
himself. When he had a complicated make-up, a
strange accent, a different walk, a new costume to be
devised, then his mimetic genius and his superbly
creative imagination flourished, devising more and
more intriguing ideas to build up, detail by fascinating detail, an entirely new personality. His Svengali,

75

his Beethoven, his Colonel Newcombe, his Malvolio, his Nero, his Zakkuri, his Micawber, these were masterpieces of purely creative acting, the plays being reduced to mere vehicles in which he could display yet another facet of that enthralling creation—himself.

But with Higgins, none of this applied: no accent, no disguise, no costume, no mannerisms. All he had to do was to walk on to the stage wearing modern everyday clothes without any make-up and speak Shaw's lines exactly as they were written down for him in his normal everyday voice without any actor's tricks whatsoever. This, Shaw repeatedly assured him, was what the play required and to do any more would spoil it. This had never happened to him before—in fact he hadn't appeared in modern clothes on the stage for twenty years—and he was completely bewildered by it. For the first time in his life he was confronted by something which he just didn't understand: a completely straight part in which no *acting*, as he understood it, was wanted—or permitted. Here was the chief source of friction between him and Shaw. He wanted to elaborate and embroider the part but Shaw bluntly refused. 'Stop acting, Sir Herbert, for heavens sake, stop acting. Just say the lines —*if* you can remember them,' Shaw would shout loudly. 'I do know my lines,' complained Tree, pained and embarrassed, 'I *do*, I *do*, really I do.' Shaw fixed a ferocious glare at the quivering man. 'I don't dispute that for a moment, Sir Herbert,' he said. 'I admit that you do know *your* lines—but you don't know *mine*!' Once again, the retinue enjoyed that one very much.

On another occasion, while rehearsing the second act, Tree grasped a walking stick and limped across the stage. 'May I ask just what the devil you think you're doing with that walking-stick, Sir Herbert?' asked Shaw in astonishment.

Tree turned to explain: 'You see, Shaw, I think Higgins drinks a lot of port, bachelors frequently do, haven't you noticed that? Therefore the probability is that he would have gout therefore he would walk with a limp. Hence the walking-stick. It's quite simple.'

'Why stop at a limp and a stick?' asked Shaw with ferocious sarcasm. 'Why don't you put a patch over one eye, have one leg and a parrot on your shoulder, then we can do *Treasure Island*?' But it was fatal to make sarcastic suggestions to Tree, however outrageous, for he was sure to adopt them. '*Treasure Island*,' he murmured thoughtfully, 'hmmmmm, yes . . . yes . . .' and you could see that he was already playing Long John Silver in front of an audience of terrified children. 'Dana, Dana,' he called, 'what are we doing next Christmas?' Henry Dana appeared at the side of the stage like a jack-in-the-box. 'You did suggest a revival of *Pinkie and the Fairies*,' he said. Tree looked blank. 'Whatever is that?' he enquired. 'It's that children's play which Mr Robertson wrote for us five years ago,' explained Dana. Tree grimaced, and shuddered. 'All those children . . . oh, for an hour with Herod.' The retinue, who had heard this one before, laughed loudly and applauded. 'No,

Dana, I think not,' said Tree sadly, 'you know what Pinkie can do to those fairies, Pinkie can **** the fairies . . . Sorry, Mrs Campbell, mere alliteration, so natural to a poet . . . No, Dana, we'll do *Treasure Island* instead.'

Other suggestions for making Higgins an interesting personality flowed in thick and fast. 'I'm convinced that Higgins is under a great strain, Mr Shaw, so he'd have a twitch,' said Tree hopefully one day. 'It's a little thing like that which shows temper, which he's got, and the nervous strain of making good his boast. You wouldn't know about these things, Mr Shaw, being an amateur, but this is how we professionals work. And surely he would vault on to the piano from time to time?'

'Why?' asked Shaw.

'Because he's one of those men who is physically restless,' replied Tree. 'Like this, let me show you.' Suiting the action to the word, Tree took a little run at the piano, and lifted himself to the top where he lay at full length, panting with the strain. He looked hopefully at Shaw who was shaking his head.

'No,' said Shaw. 'I wouldn't consider it. You're too old, Sir Herbert, far too old.'

Disappointed, Tree lowered himself gingerly to the ground. Then another idea struck him. 'Surely he'd take snuff, perennial bachelors usually do, it's a charming eighteenth-century touch, don't you think? And surely he'd speak with a slight Scots accent?'

'Why, Sir Herbert?' asked Shaw in astonishment.

'Because the Scots speak the best English in the

78

world. I'm sure that if you were to look into his background you'd find that his grandparents were born in Aberdeen.'

'I'm aware that the Scots make this boast, Sir Herbert,' replied Shaw patiently, 'a similar claim is also made by the inhabitants of Boston. Why don't you give Higgins an American accent?'

'Yes,' said Tree, delighted, 'I will, just listen . . .'

'STOP!' thundered Shaw. 'I should have known better than to suggest it. Now, Sir Herbert, I am a reasonable man. If you would like to demonstrate all these little elaborations I will give you my honest opinion of them and if they don't make the proper theatrical effect then I will say no.'

Tree was delighted to be thus challenged. He took up the walking-stick, and reciting Higgins's speech in Act Two, 'Eliza, you are going to remain in this house for the

(*The Graphic*)

79

next six months,' he took a pinch of snuff and limped round the stage reciting the speech in a broad Scots accent, his face twitching like a maniac. The company crowded round watching curiously. When he had finished, he turned eagerly to Shaw who had collapsed into his stall shaking with laughter. Mrs Pat was in a similar condition. The company did not presume to join in but their amused smiles and glances told their own story.

'Well, Sir Herbert, if that's what you call being a professional then I'm very glad I'm an amateur,' said Shaw, wiping the tears away from his eyes. 'I'm sorry but it really won't do. Higgins does not take snuff, nor does he limp, nor does his face twitch, nor does he speak in a Scots accent. Forget all this nonsense, Sir Herbert, it's only confusing you. Just say the lines as I've written them. They've been written with great care because despite what you may think, I do know my job. Say the lines. Just say them. It's only a matter of technique.'

'Oh, but I haven't *got* any technique,' moaned Tree petulantly, 'I *hate* technique! It does destroy the inspiration so *dreadfully*!' Therein lay the root of the trouble, for the creative imagination cannot be thus easily suppressed, and Tree's was never more fertile than when faced with what he took to be an empty canvas which urgently needed filling.

Shaw sternly refused all further suggestions, but another source of tension soon appeared. Tree began to be haunted by a nagging suspicion that he had chosen the wrong part, a very distressing matter as any miscast actor knows full well. He suddenly decided that after all he would like to play Doolittle, the Dustman, one of Shaw's most inspired creations, certainly his finest show-stealing small part. Tree's decision was largely due to the fact that it was, in rehearsal, receiving such a fine performance from Edmund Gurney. This middle-aged Irishman (he had been born in Cork) had, like Forbes Robertson, started life as a painter and had made a late entry in the theatre. He quickly made a name for himself in the provinces as a robust character comedian, but it was his performance as the tormented, neurotic Dr Blenkinsop in the original production of *The Doctor's Dilemma* which had brought him to Shaw's notice. 'To Edmund Gurney who made more of the character of Dr Blenkinsop than I ever did,' was Shaw's flattering inscription to his fellow Irishman written in the presentation copy of the published play. He later played Snout in Tree's production of *A Midsummer Night's Dream* and thus arrived at the *Pygmalion* rehearsals, known to and admired by his author and his manager and with the part of a lifetime in his hands.

Gurney was one of those hard-working, reliable professional actors who give a good reading at the first rehearsal and then slowly but surely build up from there getting a little better each day. He was one of the few actors (Ernest Thesiger rehearsing the Dauphin in *Saint Joan* ten years later was another) who received Shaw's supreme accolade. 'I have a strong temptation, Mr Gurney,' Shaw said to him after the first rehearsal, 'to tell you to go away and not come back till the dress-rehearsal, for there's nothing *I* can add to your performance!' Gurney, like Mrs Pat, would go into the streets and markets and watch and listen to the dustmen at work; he also attended debates in the House of Commons and listened attentively to Lloyd George's speeches in order to acquire the right flavour of contempt for the aristocracy, after Shaw had admitted that there was a great deal of Lloyd George in Doolittle. 'Lloyd George would sell you a peerage for £50,000 as quickly as Doolittle would sell you his daughter for £5,' was Shaw's comment. Gurney's performance in rehearsals was so good and so funny that even the actors and the stage-hands watching it from the wings would be helpless with laughter. They never did that when Tree was rehearsing Higgins; to be envious was only human, and Tree was exceedingly human.

Admittedly there were only two scenes, but they

(The Sketch)

were deliciously amusing, and the last act entrance in the wedding clothes was well calculated to cause a sensation. There was the cockney accent, the dustman's clothes, the grimy impoverished face, the bad breath, a whole range of physical mannerisms to be devised—yes, the part had tremendous possibilities. So one day Tree took Shaw aside and rather pathetically asked if he could play Doolittle. Shaw looked at him in amazement.

'But what about Mr Gurney,' he said. 'He's under contract to play the part. What will he say? What will you do with him?'

Tree was prepared for this and had his answer ready. 'Let him play Higgins,' he said grandly. 'He'll be delighted. He'll be an excellent Higgins. He's such a good actor, as you know, he's got plenty of *technique*.' But Shaw had rather been expecting a situation like this, and he knew how to deal with it. 'No, it won't do, really it won't,' he said, turning on the full power of his Irish charm. 'You are Sir Herbert Beerbohm Tree, actor-manager of the beautiful His Majesty's Theatre and the acknowledged King of the English stage. You have a large and adoring public who travel long distances and pay large sums of money to see *you*, Sir Herbert, to enjoy and taste to the full those enthralling and bewitching displays of the actor's art which are your unique speciality. You really shouldn't play a secondary part in your own theatre, however good it may be. It would disappoint your public, and that would never do, would it now?'

'No . . . no . . . I see what you mean . . . of course not. . . .' Tree nodded his agreement. Shaw pressed his point home like the skilled tactician he was. 'Persevere with Higgins, Sir Herbert. It's coming—slowly, I admit, but it's coming.' This cunning appeal to Tree's vanity was not made in vain: He saw the wisdom of it and the question of his playing Doolittle was never mentioned again.

So he returned to Higgins and did his best to impersonate this elusive and unattractive person, a professor of phonetics. Now it so happened that he had never met or even heard of such a person, his own diction being just like the rest of him, like nothing on earth. But now a further source of trouble became evident. At heart Tree was a romantic and an incurable sentimentalist: it seemed to him natural and inevitable that if a play had a hero, he should love and eventually marry the heroine of it. The cold, cynical realism of Shaw's last act baffled and saddened him. So he did his best to make Higgins sympathetic in the character of a lover, for which Shaw had left so little space that he was completely baffled—until inspiration came to his rescue. 'Supposing, after Eliza goes off at the end of the fifth act, supposing . . . just supposing I were to go on to the balcony and throw flowers to her,' he suggested brightly. 'It would be rather a charming way of finishing off the play, don't you think?' 'You'll finish it,' said Shaw darkly. 'No!' Tree looked crestfallen. 'But it might be rather amusing if . . .' he pressed hopefully, but as usual Shaw had the last word. 'Sir Herbert, I have made it painfully clear that Higgins may be dependent on Eliza but he does NOT love her, nor she him. If you throw those flowers, it will contradict everything that has been said in the last act. No flowers!'

Tree's determination to play Higgins on romantic lines provoked Shaw to one of his most memorable insults. 'I say, Tree,' he shouted when Tree was rehearsing the fifth act, 'must you be so damned *Tree-acly*!!??' This was said in front of the entire company, all the stage-staff and all of Tree's retinue. Everybody in earshot froze in horror, except for a few who were in convulsions of mirth like the electrician who laughed so much he fell off his ladder. Stanley Bell and Henry Dana looked at each other aghast—you just didn't address remarks like that to the Chief in his own theatre; instant death should have been Shaw's punishment. Tree nearly had an apoplectic fit: he turned purple and burst into tears. 'I can't go on,' he sobbed, 'I really can't face it. I'll have to cancel this play and put on *Trilby* instead . . . Oh God, what have I *done* to deserve this. . . .' Mrs Pat led him gently to the stage door and tried to comfort him. After several gulps of fresh Haymarket air had calmed him down, after she had reassured him that it was only a *joke*, that no slur was intended on his beautiful acting and that he knew by now what Shaw was like, she returned to the stage where Shaw was continuing with the two understudies.

'Oh, how could you, Mr Shaw,' she raged, 'it's

simply outrageous! Don't you realize that Sir Herbert is risking his reputation and fortune to put on your play and paying you, incidentally, a handsome sum in the process, and all you can do is to insult him with a sickly suburban pun like that. And you have the insolence to say to everybody that *I* am impossible in the theatre!'

It was too much. Shaw collapsed on to his chair and started to shake and shriek with laughter. Mrs Pat gazed furiously at him and then proceeded to lose her temper. 'If Mr Shaw does not leave the theatre this *instant*,' she screamed, 'then *I* will. And I will NOT come back!!' Shaw pulled himself together, gazed imperturbably at her for a moment, pulled himself together and then, with supreme dignity, gathered up his papers, notebook, torch, pencil, spectacles and script and, after courteously bowing to Mrs Pat, walked out of the theatre through the back of the stalls. But even before he had gone, Mrs Pat was continuing with the rehearsal. 'My aunt died of influenza, so they say,' she recited to Carlotta Addison, Margaret Bussé and Algernon Greig who made up the Eynesford-Hill family. Shaw stopped in his tracks and turned to face the stage. 'Wretched woman,' he thundered, 'can you not even wait till I've gone?'

If Tree tried to make Higgins romantic, Mrs Pat fell into another and equally unfortunate artistic trap —she tried to make Eliza too funny, broadening and emphasizing what should have been subtle, not realizing that the humour was in the lines and not in the

Sir Herbert Beerbohm Tree as Professor Higgins, painted by
Charles Buchel. Buchel painted portraits of Tree in all his great
roles. The walls of the Dome were covered with them (his King
John hangs today in the foyer of Her Majesty's Theatre).

Left: Lilli Marberg was the first Eliza, at the Hofburgtheater in October 1913.

Below: Frau Tilla Durieux was the second Eliza, and she played it at the Lessing Theatre, Berlin 1913.

One of Mrs Pat's favourite photographs of herself which appeared in all the glossy magazines after she became Mrs Cornwallis-West.

A remarkable group picture. Lady Randolph Churchill had written a play, *His Borrowed Plumes,* and here she is (bottom right) with the company which included Mrs Pat (centre), her daughter Stella (top right), Henry Ainley (top left) and George Cornwallis-West (back centre).

Mrs Pat as Eliza, His Majesty's Theatre, 1914, Act I (left), Act III (right). These pictures appeared in the now defunct weekly *The Illustrated Sporting and Dramatic News*.

Right: 'My aunt died of influenza—so they said.' The famous tea party. Carlotta Addison (Mrs Eynesford-Hill), Mrs Pat, Margaret Bussé (Clara Eynesford-Hill).

Below: Edmund Gurney as Doolittle concealing his top hat under the sofa in Act V.

Left: 'Covent Garden! What a darned thing!' Tree as Higgins remembers where he met the Eynesford-Hills. Algernon Greig as Freddy in the background.

Below: 'Blimey, it's Eliza!' Act II. Edmund Gurney, Mrs Pat, Tree.

Edmund Gurney as Doolittle,
taken in New York, 1914.

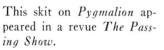

One of the many cartoons which appeared shortly after the première.

This skit on *Pygmalion* appeared in a revue *The Passing Show*.

Theatrical cartoonery was at its
height in 1914, as the liveliness of
these two sheets clearly indicates.

Mrs PEARCE

Am I like this?!!
Geraldine Oliffe

July. 14. '14

"Such bloody"
nonsense.
but still.
Yours sincerely
Irene Delisse.

CRIMINALS
I HAVE MET
Stanley Bell
14/7/14

These drawings by Margaret Bussé, who played Clara, were made from the wings of the theatre during the brief London run. As Geraldine Oliffe, Irene Delisse and Stanley Bell did not appear on the production photo, these drawings are the only record of them.

Right: This drawing of Mrs Pat is one of the rare occasions when she signed herself Stella Corn-wallis-West.

LIZA DOOLITTLE

A contemporary picture of Shaw making production notes, taken during the final dress-rehearsal.

Above: Marion Terry as Mrs
Higgins and the cricket-playing
C. Aubrey Smith as Higgins.
Aldwych Theatre 1920.

Right: Mrs Pat as Eliza, Aldwych Theatre 1920. Note how
different is her flower-girl costume from the one she wore in
1914.

Right: Eliza Keefe, the famous
Charing-Cross flower-girl, waiting in the pit queue for the first
performance of *Pygmalion,*
April 11th 1914.

Left: His Majesty's Theatre and the Haymarket as they were round about 1900.

Below: The interior of the theatre.

The last years. Mrs Pat and Moonbeam in Paris 1938.

performance, a predictable mistake for one inexperienced in playing comedy. Shaw was constantly pulling her up on this point. 'Don't make faces,' he would say, but the moment his back was turned Mrs Pat would impishly put her tongue out at him and continue as before. Once, Shaw became so irritated with her that he actually went on his knees and begged her to act the way he wanted. 'Stella,' he pleaded, 'you are the MOST exasperating and impossible woman I've ever known. You musn't overplay the comedy in this scene, or you'll kill it stone dead. You mustn't laugh or pull silly faces which aren't a bit amusing anyway, and you mustn't find the scene funny because if you do then the audience won't.' Mrs Pat gazed down at him fondly. 'Aaaaaaah, that's where I like to see my authors,' she crooned, 'on their knees at my feet.' She started to stroke his head and then looked closely at the iron-grey hair. 'Why, Bernard, you have another white hair in your head. Fancy!!' Shaw scrambled angrily to his feet. 'And who put it there, Stella,' he roared, 'who put it there, just you tell me that?!'

Some of Shaw's rehearsal methods were a little odd to his temperamental stars. Instead of giving verbal comments to the assembled company at the end of rehearsals, as was the standard method in other theatres, he would write his comments on little pieces of paper and distribute them individually. Neither Tree nor Mrs Pat appreciated this: Tree invariably threw his notes away, but Mrs Pat, while she usually read and remembered their contents, had her own comment to make. 'Thank you, Mr Shaw,' she once said acidly, 'I can always find a good use for a little piece of paper.' Sometimes, when Shaw spoke to her really sharply, she would rush off the stage and walk up and down in the darkness of the wings, sulking. On one such occasion, a young actor who happened to be in earshot, overheard her muttering to herself. 'He knows nothing, that old man with the beard,' she was saying, 'that old man with the beard, he knows *nothing*. NOTHING!!' Greatly alarmed, the young actor approached her nervously. 'Surely . . . surely . . . you can't be referring to Mr Bernard Shaw?' he stammered. She looked at him with smouldering, contemptuous eyes. '*So he says!!*' was her cryptic reply, which left the scandalized young actor wondering for a wild, lunatic moment, just *who* was masquerading behind that famous white beard.

And there were times when she complained bitterly about not having enough to do in the play, particularly at the beginning of Act Four when she was required to sit quietly on the side of the stage while Higgins and Pickering gleefully discussed her success at the ball. 'I just *sit* here,' she wailed, 'and I do *nothing*. It's ridiculous. The audience will think I've gone to sleep!' Shaw considered this criticism for a moment. 'Well, I'll tell you what I'll do,' he said brightly, 'I'll get Sir Herbert to come over and *pat* you once in a while, how would that do, eh?' Mrs Pat grimaced and shook her head sadly. 'I *hate* being patted,' she moaned in a charnel-house voice.

There were times when Tree, irritated beyond endurance, would rush about the theatre, his arms raised to heaven, screaming—literally screaming—with despair and frustration. And there were days when they would not even speak to each other; a brooding hostile silence reigned over the theatre like a black fog, and messages had to be passed through the long-suffering Henry Dana. . . . 'Dana, will you please tell Mrs Campbell that if she insists on draping herself over the piano in that absurd Pre-Raphaelite posture, the occupants of the stage box will not be able to see me?'. . . 'Mr Dana, will you be so good as to inform Sir Herbert that if he insists on eating an apple as noisily as he does in my big speech, I shall start

Sir Herbert during
someone else's scene.

playing the piano during his?' 'Mr Dana, I wonder if you would be so kind as to convey my most respectful compliments to Sir Herbert and to Mrs Campbell and warn them that if they don't learn the lines I have written specially for them, I shall regretfully have to withdraw this play from production at His Majesty's Theatre, and give it to Sir George Alexander and Miss Irene Vanbrugh, who *really* appreciate me!'

★

But it was not always rows and sarcasm and tears. There were happy days when it was all sweetness and light: when good and fruitful work was achieved in an atmosphere of friendliness and optimism. Then Tree would sweep Shaw and Mrs Pat off to lunch in the private room at the Garrick Club. The conversation on these occasions would bubble and sparkle most entertainingly, for these were three supremely witty and intelligent people who only needed good food and wine and an appreciative audience to spark each other off. The audience, which Tree took good care to provide could include anybody who had caught Tree's attention that day, and being a truly democratic and unsnobbish person, it didn't matter how lowly or unimportant they were—it could be a small-part actress or a stage-hand or an understudy, or even the call-boy—anybody whom he liked and who promised to be a good listener. It was a great privilege to be included in one of those luncheon parties and from the memories, both written and verbal, of those happy few, it has been possible to reconstruct some of the triumvirate's more memorable table-talk.

Mrs Pat would ponder at length over the menu; she had an enormous appetite and this was the heyday of Edwardian gastronomy when large, rich meals were the fashion. 'Onion soup and then a little smoked salmon, I adore smoked salmon when it's really *expensive*,' she said to the waiter, 'then perhaps an avocado stuffed with shrimps, then a little breast of chicken with some of those *adorable* little button mushrooms, then some dover sole and perhaps a meringue glacée to finish off with and some purple grapes.'

'Mrs Campbell, *how* can you possibly eat a meal like that in the middle of a working day?' asked Shaw, gazing at her in astonishment. 'Let me give you a solemn warning—you'll get so fat that nobody will ever employ you, and that will be the judgement of heaven on you for your greediness. You'll never act again, except, perhaps Boadicea.'

'I would *love* to play Boadicea,' replied Mrs Pat enthusiastically, 'there's great fulfilment in a sword and breastplate.'

'Then you must play St Joan,' replied Shaw resignedly, 'I'm planning to write a play about her.'

'Why do you want to write a play about St Joan?' asked Tree in bewilderment.

'To protect her from John Drinkwater,' said Shaw. Tree considered this. 'Yes, there are distinct possibilities, we could get Sargent to design my armour, all those battles, gold and black would be rather intriguing . . . she gets burned at the stake, doesn't she? Yes, that would be most amusing . . . perhaps there could be a scene in Heaven . . . I might play St Peter . . .'

'I haven't written it yet,' said Shaw firmly, 'but I can tell you one thing—there will NOT be a scene in heaven and you will NOT play St Peter. Now, Sir Herbert, will you please give the waiter your order because Mrs Campbell is visibly starving for her little snack, and you know she must keep up her strength.'

'Aaaah, yes, food,' murmured Tree to the young waiter as he scanned the menu, 'a loaf of bread, a glass of wine, but not thou . . .' The waiter was not used to people like Tree. 'Yes, sir,' he said, 'red or white wine?' Tree found this irresistibly amusing and chuckled delightedly with the rest. 'My dear fellow,' he said charmingly to the waiter, 'you really must not believe a single word either I or anybody at this table says. . . Mind you, Shaw, if Dana had his way, that's what I'd be eating every day. He keeps on telling me I'm extravagant . . . *me*, extravagant?' And he laughed at the absurdity of it all. 'Well, I fancy I'm in rather a Pickwickian mood today, I'll settle for a large and amusing chop with tomato sauce.'

'My needs are equally simple,' said Shaw, 'I'll have a simple cheese salad with a four-minute soft-boiled egg, a sliced tomato without the skin, some lettuce hearts with raisins and salted peanuts, one thick slice of whole-meal brown bread with salted butter, an apple and a glass of milk.'

'Nursery food,' said Mrs Pat scornfully, 'I can't imagine how you can live on such an infantile diet.'

'Well, Mrs Pat,' said Tree heartily, 'shall we give Shaw a beefsteak and put some red blood in him?'

'For heavens sake, *don't*, Sir Herbert,' she replied with a shudder. 'He's bad enough as he is, but if you give him red meat, then no woman in London will be safe!'

But Tree could not forget the theatre for long; his mind was never far from it, no matter what was being discussed. 'Red . . . red . . . yes, that would be a good colour for my second act smoking jacket—or should it be purple? Purple with gold frogging, perhaps? Now you should wear red, Mrs Campbell. Your ball-dress in Act Four, there are distinct possibilities in red.'

'Red is a colour I abominate,' said Mrs Pat with a grimace, 'it makes me look like a horrid little *letter-box*.'

'Well, we certainly don't want that,' said Tree heartily, 'you know how I loathe competition. But I want you to look your best and wear something very splendid in that scene. How about that dress you wore in *False Gods*.'

'You mean that dress with black and yellow horizontal stripes?' asked Mrs Pat in astonishment. 'Oh, Sir Herbert, you can't be serious. It made me look like a very angry, very old wasp in an *interesting condition*!'

'Talking of wasps,' said Shaw, 'I've just had a very interesting proposal from that remarkably waspish American actress, Maxine Elliott. You both know her, of course?'

Mrs Pat smiled maliciously. 'Indeed I do and I think she's a very *nice* woman. So nice that if you knew her you'd even think she was a good actress.'

Tree grimaced in distaste. 'Remarkable woman,' he purred, 'but very superstitious. I believe she never sleeps more than thirteen in the bed. And never on Friday. But please don't misunderstand me. My dislike is purely platonic.'

Mrs Pat shrugged her shoulders: 'Well, I don't think it matters what people do, as long as they don't do it in the street and frighten the horses.' Shaw smiled. 'Well, I don't know if Miss Elliott frightens her horses but, my God! she certainly frightens me,' he said. 'She proposes to form a repertory company in New York and she wants to play Candida one night, Cleopatra the second, Lady Cicely the third, Mrs Dubedat the fourth. . . .'

'Four beautiful women,' interrupted Mrs Pat, 'what a pity Miss Elliott is so ugly . . . my dear, she has a mouth like Tesman's slippers.'

'Who the devil's Tesman?' inquired Tree through a mouthful of pork chop.

'Ibsen,' said Shaw. 'Hedda Gabler's husband.'

Tree shuddered: 'Ibsen . . . oh my God,' he wailed, 'People are always trying to get me to do those Ibsen plays, but really, since those dreadful matinées of—what was it—*An Enemy of the People* or something, I really don't think I can face it. Gloom, goblins and gonorrhoea, that's Ibsen. He's so boring, even the grave yawns for him.'

'I agree,' said Mrs Pat firmly. 'I have played Hedda Gabler but my Italian blood prevents me from understanding her. My Swedish masseuse could play her ten times better than me.'

Shaw chuckled. 'Give me her name and address and I'll start rehearsals tomorrow.'

Mrs Pat shrugged her shoulders. 'Useless. She has no brains.'

Shaw looked defiantly at her. 'Actresses don't need brains. They only need a good memory. Now your daughter Stella could play Hedda very well.'

There was a long pause while Mrs Pat considered this, and then she sighed deeply, and turned impulsively to Shaw. 'Oh Joey, why did we never have a child. With your brains and my beauty, it would be the perfect human being.'

'Dangerous, Stella, very dangerous,' chuckled Shaw sardonically, 'supposing it had your brains and my beauty.' Game, set and match to Shaw, but in the laughter which greeted this, Mrs Pat's was the loudest. 'Oh, Joey, you're *wicked*, *wicked*! That'll be all over the town by tonight, I know. Oh, Sir Herbert what can we do with him? If he's like this on a milk diet, what *will* he be like when I've driven him to drink, as I surely must and will? . . . Anyway, Joey, you're quite right about one thing. Repertory is the only way to act. I shall start a repertory company here in London as soon as *Pygmalion* has finished. One night I shall play Cleopatra, and the next night I shall just walk on, carrying a tray.'

It was now Tree's turn to score. 'I shall watch that tray with the greatest possible interest, Mrs Campbell,' he said, 'and I wouldn't mind having a sizeable bet that it'll have John the Baptist's head on it!'

★

Nothing remains a secret for long in the tiny, enclosed, gossip-ridden world of the West End, and stories of the internal dissensions started to be talked about outside the theatre. It quickly became an open secret that all was not well at His Majesty's: in the Garrick Club, the Green Room Club, the bars, dressing-rooms, green-rooms and pubs, anywhere where theatre people gathered, speculation and scandal flourished. Bets were taken as to whether the play would ever open, and if it did, then when? The oddest rumours began to circulate, most of them, in all probability, planted by Tree. It was said that the public was to be admitted to the rehearsals for the unheard-of sum of £10 each, that Mrs Pat was to defy the censor and say words which had definitely been banned, that she had finally walked out of the production and had gone to Aix to recover, that Shaw and Tree had actually come to blows in the stalls, that the first night list had been cancelled and the theatre was to be filled instead entirely with dustmen and flower-girls, that Tree had cancelled the whole production and proposed to fill the gap

with a revival of *David Copperfield* in which he proposed to treble the parts of Micawber, Peggotty *and*
Uriah Heep to compensate for all the non-acting
which Shaw had inflicted on him during the last two
months. In the light of all this, it was hardly surprising that the National Film Company offered £100
for the chance of making a film of a day's rehearsal.
Shaw bluntly refused and his decision was posterity's
loss.

Tree was a superb public relations officer, years
before the term or the function had officially been
invented. He adored publicity and had a genius for
getting it: having a shrewd understanding of the
news value of all the rehearsal rows, he cunningly
leaked them to the press whilst officially denying
that there had been any rows. 'It's sheer and utter
nonsense to talk of rows,' he said to the reporters
who gathered daily at the stage-door, 'Mr Shaw, Mrs
Campbell and myself are like three little birds
twittering in the trees—no pun intended, I assure
you! Mr Shaw is contributing *something* to this production I readily admit, but naturally we give and
take; that is the only basis on which we can work
successfully. I must say that Professor Higgins is
the longest and most difficult part that I have yet
played. The part is really a mixture of Bernard Shaw
and Lord Northcliffe and is, incidentally, longer
than Hamlet—or at least it seems so. I don't know
if Higgins loves Eliza, that is a profound secret in the
mind of the author; Mr Shaw might tell you. But I
don't know how Mrs Campbell feels about the matter.'

Mrs Pat's views on the subject remained a secret, for she firmly declined to be interviewed or questioned. It was not that she liked publicity any less than Tree or Shaw—she merely had a different way of getting it. Since journalistic manners were better in 1914 than they are now, her wishes were respected, though *The Times* allowed its reputation for gentlemanly behaviour to slip when it ungallantly revealed her age. 'Where is youth these days? Far from being at the helm it is lucky if it is allowed to scrub the decks. A new play is to be produced at His Majesty's Theatre. The combined ages of its author, its manager and its leading lady are 166. Sir Herbert is 60; Mr Shaw is 57; and Mrs Patrick Campbell, who plays a flower-girl of 18, is 49!'

Tree allowed the *Daily Express* to see that top secret document, the only complete script of the play; and permitted them to publish the cast list and a detailed synopsis of the plot. 'Mr Shaw has done nothing better,' commented their leader-writer, 'this is indeed a twentieth-century Galatea.' When other reporters questioned Tree about the play he replied evasively. 'Call it a comedy if you will. Shaw has many things to say but he does not go deeply into any one question. It is certainly not all talk. There is plenty of action but I'm afraid I cannot disclose whether the amount of action equals the amount of talk. You see, it is a Shaw play!'

Plans for opening in mid-March were obviously premature: the play was not nearly ready and another three weeks were surely needed. Already tempers were getting short and the company's morale was sagging. It was a debatable point as to which was the more annoying—Tree's jokes, Mrs Pat's fits of temperament or Shaw's irrepressible energy.

This last doubtless derived from the extreme frugality of his breakfast—a cup of Postum coffee and a biscuit—and the exercise he took in the early morning. He would walk briskly across St James's Park, run three at a time up the Duke of York's steps, stride down Charles Street and, with a hearty greeting to the stage-door keeper, bound through the swing doors of the theatre on to the stage. This shining figure, bursting with good health and vitality, was unspeakably irritating to Tree and Mrs Pat who, in common with most of the human race, were not at their best so early in the morning.

One day in late March, they arrived on the stage looking unusually haggard and dissipated: they had both been up late the night before. Shaw, wearing his Inverness cape and Norfolk jacket, his eyes shining and his greying beard twirling for action, strode eagerly down the stalls and leapt on to the stage. 'Good morning, good morning,' he boomed, 'and how are we all today?' Tree and Mrs Pat exchanged despairing glances. 'Good morning, Bernard,' she replied in a hollow voice. 'What do you want to do now?' Shaw thought for a moment. 'I think we'll take the love-scene in the last act and I'll watch from the back of the stalls without interrupting, and then I'll come down and tell you how bad you are,' and he laughed uproariously at this, though neither Tree nor Mrs Pat thought it was in the least funny. They struggled through the scene and it was very bad: they were both too tired, too old, and too fat. Shaw rushed down at the end, his eyes blazing. 'That's terrible,' he shouted. 'Not a bit like what I want. I don't want your flamboyant personality, Mrs Campbell. I want an ordinary London flower-girl in love.' Mrs Pat snorted contemptuously. 'Love,' she said, 'what do you know about love? One of these days you'll drink a glass of whisky and then God help all of us.'

There was another reason for the delay—the theatre was doing excellent business with a stopgap revival of *The Darling of the Gods*. This was a spectacular slice of oriental Sardoodledum in which Tree wearing a series of ravishing kimonos in the part of a sinister-charming villainous Japanese potentate, Zakkuri, leered, chuckled, soliloquized and murdered his way through the cherry-trees and snow-capped mountains of David Belasco's ancient Japan. The last week was unusually hectic with a Royal Gala performance in front of George V and Queen Mary which was broken up by a party of suffragettes demonstrating in the stalls and being noisily ejected by the police. But theatrical crisis was tactfully offset by domestic happiness: his daughter Viola, a tall handsome girl who looked very like her father and who had recently married the writer and dramatic-critic, Alan Parsons, presented Tree with his first grandson, Denys. (His brother, David Tree, born in 1915, was to play Freddie in the *Pygmalion* film some twenty-four years later. Viola herself was to make a brief but hilarious appearance in the ball-scene of the film as a very aggressive, trouser-suited journaliste.)

The première of *Pygmalion* was announced for April 11th and to allow a full fortnight of uninterrupted rehearsals for it, *The Darling of the Gods* was withdrawn on March 28th. On the last night, Tree made a brief curtain speech. 'Ladies and gentlemen, next month I am succumbing to the inevitable Bernard Shaw who will be making his first appearance in this theatre as dramatist-in-chief. I have heard an extraordinary rumour that the play has been cut in rehearsal, severely cut. This is not true. It will be played just as it came from the brain of its creator. There is another rumour that the play is cynical, and this too I would like to deny with all possible speed. It contains a new view of the Shavian spirit, but is this incompatible with gaiety and wit? I think you will find *Pygmalion* a very agreeable five-act entertainment.'

From Monday March 30th, the pressure was increased while the theatre was closed for final rehearsals. Under Shaw's eagle eye and relentless discipline, the company started the final period of hard, intensive work. In those days before British Actors Equity Association started to govern the conditions of rehearsals, actors were expected to give themselves up for rehearsals as often and as long as their employers wished, without complaint and without payment. Shaw had worked out a rehearsal schedule very carefully and called the company morning, afternoon and evening, though he never kept them after midnight. This was a refreshing change from Tree's routine under which actors were accustomed to being worked right through the night until dawn, since midnight and after was Tree's liveliest and most inventive period.

Oh my dear—my dear how silly *you* are [wrote Mrs Pat on the 30th], I told you that *I* was an utter silly-billy in that scene. You tried to help me with slow and quicker tempo, high and lower notes—(pianola effects)—but I couldn't be helped in that way—I tried changing my seat—that was no good with the others where they were and the Dustman coming down to where he did, so I remain and Merivale brings down the chair and sits opposite me—and I feel *comfortable* and *happy* and not as though I were in a railway carriage and I think you will be pleased with me. Merivale was truly grateful for the change of position—Tree thought it hurt no one and that if it pleased us both, should be given to us. Now I await YOUR APPROVAL. Bless you for all your impertinence—and fun and wit and kindness and goodness—and charm and friendliness . . . What you think of me and my poor talent I am not concerned with just now—My affection for you is sown in my heart because its roots are planted in gratitude . . . Bless you dear dear Joey—Stella.

After the storms and fury of the rehearsals, this was one of her rare moments of gentleness and affection. Alas, it did not last long; for during the penultimate week, her behaviour showed a marked deterioration, causing much comment and alarm. Her unpunctuality became worse, she seemed tired and worried, she drooped listlessly round the stage, forgot her lines and said those she remembered in a bored, disdainful voice. She denied that she was ill; she seemed to be preoccupied with some private, personal problem. What it was nobody knew though it is quite possible that Shaw suspected the truth. She refused to listen to his comments and criticisms at the end of rehearsals, but swept grandly out of the theatre into a waiting taxi leaving him to grind his teeth in impotent fury. Since he could not communicate verbally, he tried writing a letter to her, but she returned it unopened, thereby reducing him to the cunning device of enclosing a further note in a brown business envelope. By Sunday April 5th when the production was ready, the rest of the company all well on top of their parts and the first night only a week away, Mrs Pat's performance in rehearsals was so bad that it seemed that she had not given her part five minutes' serious attention.

5

POOR SIR HERBERT. FOR TWO
months, his delicately balanced nervous system had
been tortured by a series of jolts and blows; he had
been subjected to a succession of humiliations from
his unfeeling author and leading lady, and in trying
to do what Shaw wanted—and he had really tried—
he had experienced the most agonizing withdrawal
symptoms and birth pains of an entirely new sort of
artistic experience. It is difficult not to sympathize
with him over all he suffered even if it was in a good
cause. But if the wretched man felt that he had seen the
worst and that rehearsals could now proceed through
their final climactic week without further trouble,
he was due for a sharp disillusionment, for what had
passed was nothing compared with what was to come.
The final bombshell was just about to explode.

Monday April 6th, was the beginning of the last
week of rehearsals and this was the morning on
which Mrs Pat suddenly disappeared. It was young
Basil Dean, serving his apprenticeship as Tree's
assistant producer, who had the painful task of
breaking the news. One of his routine duties was to
ring up the Dome on the house telephone and tell
Tree that the company had arrived and that everything was ready for rehearsals. These normally
started at eleven a.m., but on this particular morning
there was no sign of her even as late as twelve-thirty.
Then a reporter arrived, and blurted out some news

that drove Dean quickly to the telephone. 'I'm sorry, Chief, but Mrs Campbell isn't coming today,' he said. 'She's got married.' Tree was still in bed and half asleep. 'What's that, what's that, *what* did you say?' he yawned. Dean took a deep breath. 'Mrs Campbell has gone and got married, Chief, and nobody knows when she'll be back.' There was a pause. 'Oh, my God,' was Tree's reply, in a voice of utter stupefaction and despair. But it was a simple case of delayed reaction: it took all of fifteen minutes for the full significance of the news to sink in. Tree, now fully dressed, his eyes blazing with fury stormed out of the lift and bounded on to the stage. '*Married*?' he screamed, 'M A R R I E D!? The woman's mad, absolutely mad. Oh God, *why* does she want to get married—wasn't once enough? She's supposed to be rehearsing that damned slut of a flower-girl here— with me. This is the last time she appears at this theatre, I swear to God it is.'

It was not long before he was in full possession of the facts. It appeared that the bridegroom was a Mr George Frederick Myddleton Cornwallis-West whom Mrs Pat had known casually for years as he was the brother of her great friend, Shelagh, Duchess of Westminster, and had been previously married to Lady Randolph Churchill . . . this had made him for a time Winston Churchill's stepfather and marrying him was the nearest Mrs Pat came to being Winston Churchill's stepmother. . . . He was a tall, charming, handsome, moustached, Edwardian playboy, a former Guards Officer who had travelled widely, fought in the Boer War, shot big game in Africa. He was a virile man-of-action, man-about-town and Mrs Pat loved him very much. He had some culture: he wrote a play *Pro Patria*, which enjoyed a brief run with Mrs Pat in 1917 and, as will be seen later, was not without some acting talent. Even Shaw approved of him, jokingly referring to him in subsequent letters as 'George Frederick Handel'. 'He's a braver man than I was,' was Shaw's comment on the elopement.

The marriage was kept a dark secret: nobody knew about it, neither Shaw nor Tree nor any of their families. It took place at Kensington Registry office at ten-thirty in the morning, the only witness being Mrs Pat's solicitor, Mr Bouchier Hawkesley. According to *The Times*, Mrs Pat was radiant in a black silk hat and a simple black dress trimmed with plaid ribbons and a white net vest. They had chosen to get married on that day because the divorce between Lady Randolph and Mr Cornwallis-West had only just been made absolute, and it was evident that he and Mrs Pat were so much in love that they could not bear to be unmarried a minute longer than was absolutely necessary. This was really important: *Pygmalion* was not.

After the wedding they motored into the country where they consumed large quantities of potted shrimps, muffins, china tea and hot buttered toast. The romantic spot which the eloping couple had selected for their honeymoon was the Dorset Arms Hotel, East Grinstead. They left behind a company of dismayed and bewildered actors, together with an apoplectic manager and a coldly resentful author, wondering if the production would ever take place at all. This was what the press was wondering: the story broke on Tuesday morning and all day an army of eager reporters and excited photographers laid siege to the theatre, clamouring for the facts. They certainly got them: Tree's undoubted talent for press-relations was never more evident than when there was an emergency and the story he cooked up to cover this crisis carried instant conviction. The press assembled in the dress-circle bar and while drinks and sandwiches were served, Tree made his statement.

'Gentlemen,' he said, smilingly confident and assured, 'of *course* I knew about the marriage, and I'm very happy for both of them, but naturally I was sworn to secrecy. I must point out that contrary to popular rumour there have been no quarrels between us, in fact rehearsals have progressed with the most delightful smoothness and harmony. My splendid company have worked so hard there is really nothing more to be done; the production is in excellent shape, so I have decided to give my splendid company a little holiday before the first performance; and I had suggested to Mrs Campbell that this would be an excellent opportunity to get married if she really felt that she couldn't wait until after the season's end, as I gather she couldn't . . . ha-ha-ha! . . . she will be back tomorrow, gentlemen, or the day after, so you can safely discount any rumour to the contrary.

Pygmalion will open as announced on Saturday.' It was all very, very smooth. The press swallowed the story whole, and it appeared in the midday and evening editions on the same day.

Naturally, the company did not get any holiday: they rehearsed as usual with Mrs Pat's understudy, a pretty young actress from Australia called Elsie Mackay. For three days, Tree and Shaw and the company were on tenterhooks with no knowledge of her whereabouts or intentions. Bets were taken in the Garrick and Green Room Clubs as to whether she would return to the production and if so, when. Fleet Street and the West End held its collective breath in anxiety, but on Thursday evening the tension was sharply relieved. Mrs Pat condescended to return to the theatre just in time for the final dress-rehearsal which had been called for six o'clock. She reappeared as suddenly as she had vanished, descending from her taxi as if from a coronation coach, swathed in expensive furs, smothered in expensive perfume and clutching armfuls of expensive flowers—and her latest pekinese, Pinky Panky Poo. Once again it was Basil Dean who had to relay the news over the house telephone. 'She's back, Chief,' he stammered. This time there was no delay; Tree came down immediately in the lift, strode through the swing-doors and out on to the pavement. He was almost incoherent with fury.

'I demand an immediate explanation of your outrageous and extraordinary behaviour, Mrs Patrick Campbell.'

'I'm Mrs George Cornwallis-West now,' she replied calmly.

'What the devil do you mean by going off and getting married without asking me, without even telling me . . . what possessed you . . . what . . . what . . .!'

'Oh, Sir Herbert,' said Mrs Pat dreamily, 'you've never in your life seen anything *like* him. George is a *golden* man! He's six foot four and *everything in proportion*.'

'But marriage . . . I mean, it's absolutely. . . .'

'I'll tell you what marriage is, Sir Herbert, and with the experience of two husbands I know what I'm talking about,' she replied happily. 'Marriage is the deep, deep peace of the double bed after the hurly-burly of the chaise-longue.' Then her mood changed and she looked at him irritably. 'Well, what are we waiting for? Don't you know the rehearsal begins at six and it's now ten past? And that we're supposed to be opening on Saturday? Don't let's waste any *more* time!' and, like an eighteenth-century galleon in full sail, she swept into the theatre and on to the stage. This was possibly the only time in his loquacious and inventive life that Tree was rendered completely speechless. 'I'm not really being unreasonable,' she said to Tree later, when they were once more on speaking terms, 'not exactly *unreasonable*! There are two whole days before we open, which I consider plenty of time for a dress-rehearsal. After all, it's *only* a dress-rehearsal!'

The dress-rehearsal lasted until three in the

morning and took place in front of an invited
audience which included two of Shaw's old sparring
partners, that eager theatregoer, G. K. Chesterton,
and H. G. Wells. In obedience to the ancient and
sacred theatrical tradition, it was unspeakably dreadful, progressing from one disaster to another.
Stanley Bell had devised a downpour of real water
for the storm in Act One. Basil Dean's suggestion
that the same effect could be achieved much more
simply by the judicious use of light and sound had
been firmly suppressed. Shaw wanted a real splash
and Tree, of course, adored realism, however cum-
bersome. Unhappily the rain-curtain, taking its cue
from the stars, decided to be temperamental and
refused to work. A resourceful stage-hand took a
wrench, and gave the stopcock a mighty twist, at
which point the water spurted out in all directions,
soaking Tree completely. He was furious and sulked
for the rest of the night. On Friday, Shaw called a
word-rehearsal which lasted from eleven in the
morning till seven in the evening. Sitting in the
middle of the dress-circle, he made copious notes in a
little notebook by the light of a small pocket torch
and twirled his beard nervously every time somebody made a mistake. There were many, and none
of them passed unnoticed.

The press was keeping an eager eye on the theatre
and every time Shaw passed through the stage-door,
he was pestered by reporters. Angrily, he refused to
make statements or answer questions, but it was a
pretty girl from the *Observer* who succeeded where

her hard-boiled male competitors had failed. 'Well, really,' he said, 'there's nothing in particular to say about *Pygmalion*. It's already been translated into German, Swedish, Polish, and Hungarian and has been performed with monotonous and unbroken, success in Germany, Vienna, Stockholm, Prague, Warsaw, Budapest—and the German section of New York.'

'How marvellous,' she gushed.

'Not a bit of it,' he replied sternly, 'there must be something radically wrong with the play if it pleases everybody but at the moment I cannot find what it is.'

'What would you say was the purpose of the play?'

'Very simple: to boil the pot. I call it a romance because it is the story of a poor girl who meets a gentleman at a church door and is transformed by him into a beautiful lady. That is what I call a romance. It is also what everybody else calls a romance, so for once we are all agreed. She does not marry anybody. I draw the line at that. She can marry whom she pleases when the curtain comes down, but I have something better for her to do when it is up. Besides, it would be highly illegal: she's already married. She got married last Monday.'

'Are Sir Herbert and Mrs Pat going to be any good as the Lady and Gentleman?' The wording of this question was careless; Shaw knew how to be tiresome and pedantic when he wanted. 'Good?' he said, 'I cannot tell you that. But I see no reason to fear a sudden change in their characters from appearing in any play of mine. Others have done so before now without moral ruin.'

'No,' she corrected herself hastily, 'by good, I mean, will they act their parts well?' Shaw shrugged his shoulders. 'I can only say that they have a reputation for doing so, and as far as I know they mean to act up to their reputation. They will doubtless do their best to please you.'

'No,' said the girl, 'I didn't mean that either. What I meant was . . . would you say that their parts are well suited to their personalities?'

'No,' exploded Shaw loudly. 'Mrs Patrick Campbell is not accustomed to selling flowers in the Charing Cross Road, nor is she in the habit of expressing herself in broad cockney. Mr Edmund Gurney's private pursuits are not those of a dustman. Sir Herbert's part is monstrously unsuited to him. He's never acted anything like this before. He didn't know how to play it. He didn't want to play it. But I persuaded him to try and now he hardly knows himself.' Shaw paused and chuckled. 'It's a funny thing, but people are always telling an actor-manager that he can't act and he eventually comes to believing it. That is what drives him to Shakespeare. Good morning.' and he raised his hat and prepared to depart, but the young girl had learned something about persistence and obstinacy from her male colleagues. 'Just one last question,' she begged with a winning smile, 'please, Mr Shaw. Will this production be based on the Continental production? The one in Vienna?'

'Certainly not, young lady,' said Shaw very firmly, 'nobody in London has seen it. In Vienna they think that Inigo Jones's church in Covent Garden is St Paul's Cathedral. They also believe that the steps of that edifice command a comprehensive view of the British Museum, the Tower of London, Westminster Abbey, and Marble Arch. Sir Herbert has finally abandoned his intention of outshining the Imperial Hofburgtheater in splendid and spacious scenery. The British fleet in the Thames and a fleet of buses on the Embankment (in the Viennese production, these are all visible from the steps of St Paul's) are the other features we have abandoned because the London County Council will allow us only one taxi-cab. It's number, incidentally is GBS N2o—this last being the scientific formula for laughing gas—a charming piece of comic fantasy by Sir Herbert. The taxi does not run over anybody—at least, not intentionally. But there is, of course, no saying what may happen before we are done. Sir Herbert does not drive the taxi but Mrs Campbell very courageously rides in it, if that is any satisfaction to you.' The interview was over. Shaw raised his hat courteously and returned to Adelphi Terrace while the girl, hugging her notebook, rushed back to the *Observer* offices in Tudor Street.

On the Saturday morning, Shaw sent two tickets by messenger to Winston Churchill, another sparring partner. They had known each other casually for years and a state of what can be described as affectionate hostility existed between them. Shaw's letter, which accompanied the tickets, was calculated to be the red rag to the bull. 'My dear Churchill,' he wrote, 'I am sending you a couple of tickets for the first performance of *Pygmalion*. Bring a friend—if you have one.' Churchill was not slow to meet the challenge. 'My dear Shaw,' he wrote as he returned the tickets, 'I deeply regret that I am unable to attend the first performance of *Pygmalion*, but I will gladly attend the second—if you have one!'

It was the now defunct *Pall Mall Gazette* which succeeded in provoking Shaw to speaking on a subject on which he had always held strong and unconventional views—laughter in the theatre, for which he had a passionate hatred. 'Will the first night audience give the play a chance? Will the hygienic gentleman who has been told by his doctor that there is nothing better for the lungs than a hearty five-minute guffaw, will he be there? Will the kindly people who think it helps the poor dear actors to be interrupted at every tenth word by shouts of appreciation, will they be laid up with influenza, as I dearly hope they may? If not, you can put all ideas of an artistic performance clean out of your head. The continuity of the play will be lost: the subtle transition from one mood to another will be obliterated. The actors trying to concentrate on a long and difficult work will be distracted and forced to give up all attempts at fine work in despair. The spectators will be worried by their own noisy enjoyment; they will miss their trains and get home, hours late, cross and tired. I suppose we shall have the usual well-intended riot which is the disgrace of the English theatre. Laughter is merely a bad habit: why can't people laugh silently, like old Weller in *Pickwick*? I tell you, *Pygmalion* will last till church time on Easter Sunday morning unless the regular first-nighters contain their tears and cheers and laughter until the ends of the acts. And if that doesn't happen, then in future I'll cut all the best bits out of my plays and thus get the whole tiresome business finished in five minutes flat . . . but I'll naturally give copies of the complete play to the critics!'

After the last rehearsal, Shaw went home and wrote his famous *Final Orders* letter to Mrs Pat. It is a most remarkable document, unique in theatrical history, and could well be subtitled 'The Intelligent Woman's Guide to Playing Eliza Doolittle.' It is worth quoting in full because of the artistic insight, brusque common sense and the sheer theatrical wisdom implicit in every sentence. It reveals more clearly than any verbal testimony the truth about Shaw as a director of plays—that he was a lynx-eyed, infinitely painstaking perfectionist, for whom no detail was too trivial to be worthy of his serious attention, and who had the talent to convey his ideas with that wit and liveliness which never deserted him.

10 Adelphi Terrace, W.C.

14th April 1914.

FINAL ORDERS
The name Nepean is in two syllables, not three; and the first 'e' is an obscure vowel, and is not to

be pronounced 'ee', but as 'a' in the phrase 'a bean'.

If you have ever said to Stella in her childhood, 'I'll let you see whether you will . . . obey me or not', and then inverted her infant shape and smacked her until the Square rang with her screams, you will . . . know how to speak the line 'I'll let you see whether I'm dependent on you'. There is a certain dragging intensity, also used in Act Four in 'YOU thank God, etc.', which is wanted here to re-establish your lead after Higgins' long speech about science and classical music and so on. The author took care to re-establish it by giving Eliza a long and energetic speech in reply to him; but the ignorant slave entrusted with the part thought she knew better than the author, and cut out the speech as useless. Now she has got to do it the other way.

On the grand finish 'I could kick myself' you retreat. The effect last night was 'Now I've spoke my piece; anitz your turn Srerbert'. You must plant yourself in an unmistakable attitude of defiance, or in some way or other *hold* him for his reply.

At the end, when Higgins says 'Oh, by the way Eliza', bridle your fatal propensity to run like Georgina to anyone who calls you, and to forget everything in an affectionate tête-à-tête with him. Imagine that he is the author, and be scornful. All that is necessary is to stop on the threshold. If you find it impossible not to come back, at least don't look obedient and affectionate. And start going away on the cue 'Eale and Binmans' so that he can shout the last sentence after you and give you an effective cue for your last word.

That smile on 'More friendly like' is developing to excess. It should be the ghastliest wannest thing, because you are just about to burst into tears; and the smile must be that sort of smile. What you have to express above all things in that speech is the torment of the woman who wants to express something that she cannot (as she thinks) express properly. Make that smile an inch wider, and you may as well stand on the points of your toes and raise your arms gracefully above your head.

I give up in despair that note of terror in the first scene which collects the crowds and suddenly shews the audience that there is a play there, and a human soul there, and a social problem there, and a formidable capacity for feeling in the trivial giggler of the comic passages. But until you get it I shall never admit that you can play Eliza, or play Shaw.

The danger tonight will be the collapse of the play after the third act. I am sending a letter to Tree which will pull him together if it does not kill him. But a good deal depends on whether you are inspired at the last moment. You are not, like me, a great general. You leave everything to chance, whereas Napoleon and Caesar left nothing to chance except the last inch that is in the hands of destiny. I could have planned the part so that nine tenths of it would have gone mechanically even if your genius had deserted you, leaving only one tenth to the Gods. Even as it is, I have forced half the battle on you; but winning half the battle will not avert defeat. You believe in courage: I say 'God save me from having to fall back on that desperate resource,' though if it must come to that it must. I don't like fighting: I like conquering. You think you like fighting; and now you will have to succeed sword in hand. You have left yourself poorly provided with ideas and expedients; and you must make up for them by dash and brilliancy and resolution. And so, AVANTI!' G.B.S.

The letter he sent to Tree consisted of eight closely written pages of abuse, advice, cajolery and cheerful insults. Unhappily, it has not survived, but what has survived, however, is Tree's comment on it. 'I'm not saying that insulting letters of eight pages are always written by madmen, but it is a most extraordinary coincidence that madmen always write insulting letters of eight pages.'

Mrs Pat read Shaw's final order at home in Kensington and sent her reply by messenger. It was brief and affectionate.

Dear Joey, all success to you tonight. It's nice to think of your friendship and your genius—I'll obey orders faithfully, I'm so thankful you carried through your giant's work to the finish—Stella.

★

To Edwardian actors and actresses preoccupied with their work, the world was a very small place, virtually limited to the parish of the West End; to Tree, Mrs Pat and the company, it had now shrunk to the four walls of His Majesty's. Not that *Pygmalion* was the only attraction that weekend, though actors and actresses rehearsing a new play in a blaze of publicity are always liable to forget this: in fact the spring season was well under way and on the evening of Saturday April 11th, many other highly desirable entertainments were available. At the Duke of York's, Godfrey Tearle and Irene Vanbrugh were loving and hating each other in the Rocky Mountains in Somerset Maugham's *The Land Of Promise*, whilst at the Strand, Lillian Braithwaite was fractionally escaping a fate-worse-than-death at the hands of Matheson Lang's unspeakable *Mr Wu*. Granville-Barker was starring in Arnold Bennett's *The Great Adventure* at the Kingsway, while his exotic and elaborate production of *A Midsummer Night's Dream* at the Savoy, boasted in Donald Calthrop the first male Puck since Elizabethan times. Lily Brayton and Oscar Asche were breaking all records at the Globe in the 365th performance of *Kismet* and Jack Buchanan was dancing his way through *Mixed Grill* at the Empire where the Grand

National was also showing on the Bioscope. There was *La Bohème* at Covent Garden and the Peer Gynt suite, the Tannhauser Overture and the Hungarian Fantasia at the Queen's Hall, conducted by Sir Henry Wood with Benno Moisewitch.

In the outside world a great many important things were happening in that second week of April. King George and Queen Mary went on a state visit to France and were rapturously received by the Parisians, and the Mexican war kicked off to a noisy start with American gunboats firing on Zapata and the rebels at Tampico. Thousands of people under Sir Edward Carson demonstrated at Hyde Park corner over the government's coercion of Ulster, Mr Winston Churchill hurried back from a yachting cruise to answer ninety-five questions in the House of Commons about the Irish situation, and the Home Rule Bill was given a second reading. Georges Carpentier knocked out England's George Mitchell of Bradford in ninety-five seconds, and Jack Johnson, world-heavyweight champion, appealed in America against his prison sentence and fine, successfully obtaining a new trial. An Italian dirigible crashed near Milan with the loss of many lives, and the Dowager Empress of Japan died in Tokyo from a heart attack under rather mysterious circumstances. Mrs Pankhurst was forbidden to address suffragettes in Dresden and a woman's boxing match was cancelled in Paris. Four gunmen were electrocuted in Sing-Sing and new evidence appeared in the case of the innocent Oscar Slater then serving a life sentence for murder which led to his subsequent release. The Penzance skating rink was destroyed by fire and Billingsgate porters complained of a distressing slump in the Good Friday consumption of fish.

But what did these things mean to Tree or Mrs Pat? What did they know or care? The play was due to open on Saturday April 11th, and that was the most important event in the world, the only one which really mattered.

'E's a gentlemen. Look at 'is boots.
(*The Sketch*)

6

THE DAY, WHEN IT FINALLY CAME,
was warm and sunny, a fact gratefully noted by
those who queued all day for the unreserved seats in
the gallery and the pit. First in the queue was
Harald Melville, the scenic designer, then a fourteen-
year-old Highgate schoolboy. It was not the accepted
theatrical custom to have premières at the end of the
week but Tree, who cared little for established customs and liked to organize matters his own way, pre-
ferred to open his new plays on a Saturday for a
number of sensible reasons. It gave him all Sunday to
relax quietly after the ordeal; it gave his glorious,
hard-working company two whole days to recover
from the tensions and agonies of the first performance and to prepare for the anti-climactical misery
of the second; and, finally, it allowed the critics a
long leisurely week-end to write those long, leisurely
notices, instead of the usual quick scramble at the
end to meet their deadline.

The curtain was due to go up at eight o'clock. By
seven-thirty the Haymarket, Pall Mall, Lower
Regent Street and Piccadilly Circus were choked
with the biggest traffic block since the Coronation,
three years earlier. Carriages, motor-cars and taxi-
cabs disgorged their splendidly dressed occupants
who streamed into the marble-paved foyer, dis-
carded their top-hats and fur coats under Charles
Buchell's portrait of Tree as King John, and pro-

gressed slowly up and down the staircase into their stall and circle seats. It was a star-studded occasion: English and Continental royalty; society and the theatrical aristocracy, the Alexanders, the Forbes Robertsons, the Wyndhams, the H. B. Irvings; everybody was there, it was an audience which gossip-columnists dream about. Shaw made a spectacular late entrance wearing a badly fitting dress-suit, a flapping Inverness cape and a bulgy blue peaked cap which made him look rather like a disgruntled French schoolboy. Disdaining the cloak-room, he thrust his rolled-up cape and cap under his seat and glowered furiously at the people round him.

Then, as now, programmes were given away free of charge on first nights, but even the closest scrutiny of its contents did not take long.

The days of the glossy, splendidly illustrated souvenir programme had not yet arrived. It is a sad and mystifying fact that although Tree was accustomed to presenting his plays with a truly lavish hand and an Olympian disregard of money, although this was a unique theatrical and social occasion, the programme which he was content to give to his privileged audience was a drab, bleak document, little more than a cast list, printed on the plainest paper and containing nothing but the essential items of information . . . the list of scenes ('what *is* a phonetic laboratory?' they could be heard saying), the programme of music to be played in what was then always described as the *entr'acte*, in which Percy

PYGMALION

A Romance in Five Acts,

By BERNARD SHAW

Henry Higgins - - - - - -	HERBERT TREE
Colonel Pickering - - - -	PHILIP MERIVALE
Freddy Eynsford-Hill - - - - -	ALGERNON GREIG
Alfred Doolittle - - - - - -	EDMUND GURNEY
A Bystander - - - - - -	ROY BYFORD
Another One - - - - -	ALEXANDER SARNER
Eliza Doolittle - - - - - -	Mrs. PATRICK CAMPBELL
Mrs. Eynsford-Hill - - - - -	CARLOTTA ADDISON
Miss Eynsford-Hill - - - - -	MARGARET BUSSÉ
Mrs. Higgins - - - - -	ROSAMOND MAYNE-YOUNG
Mrs. Pearce - - - - - -	GERALDINE OLLIFFE
Parlourmaid - - - - -	IRENE DELISSE

ACT I.

The Portico of Inigo Jones's Church of St. Paul in Covent Garden, 11.15 p.m.

ACTS II. & IV.

Professor Higgins' Phonetic Laboratory, Wimpole Street.

ACTS III. & V.

The Drawing Room in Mrs. Higgins' flat overlooking the river in Chelsea.

Act II. is on the morrow of Act I., and Act V. on the morrow of Act IV.

Some months elapse between Acts II. and III., and again between Acts III. and IV.

Period : The Present.

The Scenery by ALFRED E. CRAVEN. Acts III. & V. from designs by DENIS MACKAIL.

Programme of Music.

OVERTURE ...	...	...	"Opéra Bouffe"	...	...	...	...	*Herman Finck*
THREE ENGLISH DANCES	...	...	...	...	...	...	...	*Roger Quilter*
(a) SELENGER'S ROUND FROM OLD ENGLISH DANCES ...				...	...	...	...	*Granville Bantock*
(b) VALSE ROMANTIQUE	...	...	...	...	...	...	...	*Sibelius*
(a) TRAÜME	...	...	...	...	...	...	...	*Richard Wagner*
(b) VALSE INTERMEZZO	...	...	...	...	...	...	...	*Oscar Eve*
MOCK MORRIS AND SHEPHERD'S HEY		...	...	...	...	...	..	*Percy A. Grainger*

Mrs. Patrick Campbell's Dresses by HANDLEY SEYMOUR and Miss STONE. Other Dresses by Miss LEVERICK.
Perruquier—W. CLARKSON.

Matinée Every Wednesday and Saturday at 2.30.

Special Theatre Edition of "Thoughts and Afterthoughts," by Herbert Beerbohm Tree, can be obtained at the Box Office or from the Attendants, Price 1/-

STAGE MANAGER—STANLEY BELL. MUSICAL DIRECTOR—ADOLF SCHMID.
ASSISTANT STAGE MANAGER—ALFRED BELLEW. ASSISTANT PRODUCER—BASIL DEAN.
GENERAL MANAGER - - - - - HENRY DANA.

PRICES :—Reserved Seats : Private Boxes, £4 4s., £3 3s., and £1 11s. 6d. Stalls, 10s. 6d. Balcony Stalls, 7s. 6d.
Balcony, 5s. Upper Circle, 4s., 3s. and 2s. Unreserved Seats : Pit, 2s. 6d. Gallery, 1s.
BOX OFFICE (MR. POTTER) OPEN DAILY 10 to 10. TELEPHONE GERRARD 1777.

The safety Curtain will be lowered in the presence of the audience once during each performance.
Extracts from the Rules made by the Lord Chamberlain.—The name of the actual and responsible Manager of the Theatre must be
printed on every play bill. The Public can leave the Theatre at the end of the performance by all exit and entrance doors, which must . open
outwards. Where there is a fire-proof screen to the proscenium opening, it must be lowered at least once during every performance to ensure its
being in proper working order. Smoking is not permitted in the auditorium. All gangways, passages and staircases must be kept free from
chairs or any other obstructions whether permanent or temporary.
The Theatre has now been fitted throughout with the Ozonair System of Ventilation for the constant supply of pure fresh air, by
Messrs. OZONAIR, LTD., 96, Victoria Street, S.

Special Matinee Teas are served in the Foyer of the Theatre after each Morning Performance, consisting of freshly made Tea, cut Bread & Butter and Cake, Price 6d. per person inclusive.

WARRINGTON & CO., PRINTERS, GARRICK STREET 11·4·14.

Grainger rubbed shoulders with Sibelius and Wagner; an item about matinée teas which cost sixpence per person, and a reassuring announcement that the theatre was ventilated by Ozonair, supplied by a firm of that name on Victoria Street. There were no advertisements except for one, which was printed in a prominent place on page three; 'Special Theatre Edition of *Thoughts and Afterthoughts* by Herbert Beerbohm Tree, can be obtained at the Box Office or from the Attendants. Price 1/-.'

There was an even greater tension than usual because this was no ordinary première. When did the theatre last offer such an exciting combination of talents? The older playgoers might mumble nostalgically about the great days at the Lyceum with Irving, Ellen Terry, Forbes Robertson, Martin Harvey and Alexander, but this evening it was to be a Tree first night with its spectacle and grandeur; a Mrs Pat first night with all the scandal which that might entail—older playgoers might eagerly speculate as to which item of her clothing she would contrive to lose *this* time; and a Shaw first night with the ever-present possibility of riots and demonstrations—with Shaw you never knew *what* was going to happen.

All this speculation and uncertainty was the result of a sensational article which had appeared only that morning in the *Daily Sketch*. Tree's publicity campaign had been gathering momentum during the last two weeks with an unexpected bonus in Mrs Pat's remarriage; this had been given an excellent press coverage with the most gratifying results. By themselves, Tree, Mrs Pat and Shaw were newsworthy but together they took priority over everything else. With superb timing and a shrewd realization of its effect, Tree saved his final bombshell for that Saturday morning, and allowed it to explode in the early editions of the morning papers. The news value of *Pygmalion* can be judged from the fact that the *Daily Sketch* devoted its entire front page to pictures of Mrs Pat in her best known parts—when in modern times did a play get this sort of publicity? —together with an announcement which made the public rub their eyes with amazement and alarm over their breakfast tables.

TONIGHT'S 'PYGMALION' IN WHICH MRS PATRICK CAMPBELL IS EXPECTED TO CAUSE THE BIGGEST THEATRICAL SENSATION FOR MANY YEARS . . .

One word in Shaw's new play will cause sensation.

Mr Shaw introduces a certain forbidden word.

WILL MRS PATRICK CAMPBELL SPEAK IT?

Has the censor stepped in or will the word spread?

If he does not forbid it, then anything might happen!

It is a word which, although held by many to be merely a meaningless vulgarism, is certainly not used in decent society.

It is a word which the *Daily Sketch* cannot possibly print, and tonight it is to be uttered on the stage.

There can be little doubt of the word actually being used in the play. And this evening the most respectable audience in London is to hear that appalling word fall with bombshell suddenness from Mrs Pat's lips. This audience has been brought up on Shakespeare, but they are not yet accustomed to Shaw.

In the German version of the play which has just been published, a literal translation of the relevant dialogue is as follows:

FREDDIE: Are you going to walk across the park?

ELIZA: Walk across the park? . . . *Muck!* (Sensation.)

Literary men and women will be there from Chelsea and Hampstead and the Garden Suburb, leaders of London society, middle-class matrons and maidens, all accustomed to hearing only what is pure and clean and wholesome—and Shakespearean. It will come as a shock to the Upper Circle if they hear Mrs Pat uttering a word never before heard except from Covent Garden porters, and never before read except in the poetry of Mr John Masefield.

But if the censor does pass the word, and if the audience at His Majesty's does approve of it, then it will become the catchword of the season. And girls from Golders Green, maidens from

Maidstone, young ladies from Lewisham will all pick up this revolting epithet like the suburban girl does in the play. She shocks and distresses her mother. So will they!

In view of this announcement, it is hardly surprising that the normal tension of a first-night audience should have been increased on this occasion to a fever-pitch of nervous anticipation. As they settled down into their plush-lined stall and circle seats, their diamond tiaras, evening-gowns and stiff shirt-fronts a dazzling display, eagerly scanning their programmes for any further tit-bits of information, all topics of conversation were overridden by one which made these hardened first-nighters quiver with unsuppressed excitement—just what was The Word which Mrs Pat was going to say, and whatever It was, *would she dare to say it?*

This was a question which was giving Tree a considerable amount of anxiety. In the spacious suite on the first floor which was the Number One dressing-room, the wretched man was in a pitiful state of nerves. The careless optimism of those early rehearsal days had faded; he had now convinced himself that the play would be a dreadful failure and that Shaw's handling of the production was going to result in total disaster. But in addition to the first night terrors to which he was more than usually prone, he was now having alarming doubts about The Word. When he had embarked on the venture, it had all seemed a tremendous joke to shock the public. But that convention-defying courage had quickly dwindled when he saw the papers that morning at breakfast. For once his talent for publicity seemed to have over-reached itself—he had never expected quite such an ominously strong reaction, and his friends at the Club had shaken their heads and had prophesied disaster. 'You've gone too far this time, you'll never get away with it,' was the theme of the lunchtime conversation. The more he thought about it, the more worried he became: even though the Censor had passed it without comment, public opinion was the final censor, and it might take a very different view. There might be hostile demonstrations; they might boo; if they were *really* shocked they might even walk out or throw things. All these things had happened before and might happen again. Royalty was to be present and after all, he was a Knight Bachelor; he really should not, *could* not, take the risk of creating a nasty public scandal. The prospects were really frightening; he paced up and down his dressing-room in an agony of indecision, and it was the callboy tapping on his door and shouting 'Overture and Beginners, please. Your call, Sir Herbert,' which brought him with a sharp jerk back to the present moment. Even now it was not too late to save the situation. He left his dressing-room and went down onto the stage where the excited murmuring of the audience could be clearly heard above the tuning of the orchestra. The time was now five minutes to eight.

Mrs Pat's dressing-room had been specially erected on the stage-level to spare her the tedious necessity of going up and down the stairs for her many costume changes, and was considerably larger than the Number Two dressing-room which she would otherwise have had. For the last ten minutes she had been struggling to take off her wedding-rings which she obviously couldn't wear during the play. Neither hot water nor soap would move them an inch so she covered them with a skin-coloured tape. This produced strange ridges and lumps on her fingers provoking one critic into ecstasies over what he described as her skill in making her normally beautiful hands look bony and worn with arthritis. As Tree approached the dressing-room, she was sitting at her table in her muddy skirt and shawl and, with the aid of her dresser and a special make-up devised by Leichner, was skilfully transforming her beautifully sculptured features into those of an unwashed, grimy flower-girl.

The little incident which followed was really rather extraordinary, almost incredible, but since it was mentioned in the gossip columns of the popular press during the following week and later found its way into a number of theatrical autobiographies, and since it was also vouched for by Mrs Pat herself in her memoirs, *My Life and Some Letters*, published eight years later, it is probably true. The story has passed from mouth to mouth, is heard from old actors at parties and has thus become part of the verbal tradition of the theatre. When all the colourful details have been stripped away, the plain fact

emerges. Mrs Pat's account is brief and is banished to a footnote in her memoirs. 'Sir Herbert Tree implored me to cut the word, but, if I must say it, to say it "beautifully".' An old actor, Sydney Blow, whose memoirs were published in 1958 confirms it. 'It is difficult to imagine in those days that Tree was against her saying "bloody". He wanted her to cut it. Even on the first night he went to her dressing-room and begged her not to say it. She absolutely refused.'

By now the stage was rapidly filling up with the flower-girls and costermongers, and the gorgeously dressed opera-goers who appear at the beginning of the play. Tree's dresser, Alfred Trebell, handed him the raincoat, umbrella, notebook and pencil he required in the first scene. Tree walked on to the stage and took up his position behind one of the pillars of St Paul's Church; this moment just before the opening was always the most agonizing for him, and not all the whispers of, 'Good Luck, Chief,' from the company and stage-staff could bring a particle of comfort. The orchestra played the National Anthem, the house-lights went down, the huge, gold-fringed, red velvet curtain swept up with a heavy muffled swish and at eleven minutes past eight precisely, the English première of *Pygmalion* started.

★

Tree's fears turned out to be entirely groundless. The play went smoothly, without a single hitch: it was one of those golden evenings in the theatre when the gods were smiling happily down from their theatrical heaven and nothing could go wrong.

Alfred Craven's colourful and authentic reconstruction of Covent Garden market, with a crowd of over fifty scrambling through real rain to the shelter of the church, was given a rapturous ovation when the curtain rose on the first act. The appearance of the solitary and much publicized taxi-cab and its departure with Mrs Pat and her flower-basket was the signal for a tornado of cheers from all parts of the house. There was a buzz of keen curiosity at the contents of the Wimpole Street laboratory, and Mrs Higgins's charmingly Pre-Raphaelite sitting-room with its beautiful view of the river was loudly applauded.

As for the performances, they were, for the most part, superb. The qualification is necessary because Tree introduced, as he invariably did on first nights, an element of carefree improvisation, artfully contriving to suggest that he had actually made up some of his own lines, which in some cases he certainly had. This did not bother anybody except Shaw and the other actors—acting with Tree was well known in the Profession to be an exceptionally hazardous ordeal—for the regular patrons of His Majesty's, connoisseurs of Treedom, were quite accustomed to the spectacle of the First Gentleman of the Theatre having a little trouble with his memory. Tree had taken his usual precaution of writing out the difficult sections of his part on little pieces of paper and hiding them all round the stage: they were pinned to the backs of the columns, on to chairs and tables, on the desk, the piano and the mantlepiece. To make assurance doubly sure, he took the extra precaution of installing a team of prompters at strategic points all round the back of the stage, behind doors and windows, behind the fireplace, behind the balcony, behind the sofa, underneath the tea-table and desk, so that wherever he found himself in trouble, help would be near at hand. Not that it made the slightest difference: his stumbling and floundering was distressingly evident. However, it was generally agreed that he had caught Higgins's obstinacy, aggressiveness, brutality and childish enthusiasm with splendid conviction. He certainly had the *feel* of the part—the *words* would doubtless come later. He bumbled and dithered and roared with enormous satisfaction. He flourished his black and cerise smoking jacket with soft collar, he peeled and munched bananas, juggled with apples, vaulted on and off the piano and tried hard, oh, *so* hard, to be breezy. And if the result was not entirely convincing, one could applaud the effort if not the achievement.

When Mrs Pat made her first entrance in Act One, it was immediately clear to the company that in spite of her absence from the rehearsals and her apparent inattention during them, she really knew her part inside out. Every direction Shaw had given her was faithfully obeyed, she didn't miss a single trick; and if there were any lingering doubts as to the advisability of a middle-aged woman impersonating a young flower-girl, these were quickly swept aside when confronted by her superb comic timing and that sheer radiance of personality which only the greatest stars possess. In the rejuvenating ecstasy of her week-old second marriage, with George Cornwallis-West sitting proudly in the front row of the stalls, she achieved a dazzling youthfulness which amazed everybody: it is significant that none of the critics who saw her, and there were over sixty, were sufficiently ungallant to mention her age or to give the least hint that she was thirty years too old for the part. Although it was to deteriorate badly during the subsequent season, on that first night her performance was hailed as a truly splendid and astonishing achievement.

But much as the critics admired her, they reserved their choicest superlatives for Edmund Gurney to whom the acting honours were unanimously awarded. All his life he had waited for a part like Alfred Doolittle, the philosophical, unprincipled dustman, and when it fell into his lap, he played it with all the stops pulled out, with a splendid, heart-warming comic vitality. He delivered those long speeches which are almost operatic arias without music, with a melancholy passion and a sly cynical relish which was enormously funny, and his gloomy repetition of the catchphrases, 'middle-class morality' and 'undeserving poor' was irresistible: 'it's the jolliest stuff,' said the *Daily Telegraph*.

The great sensation of the evening was, rightly and predictably, the public utterance by Mrs Pat of the now legendary words '*not bloody likely*'. The effect of this on an audience, which had been waiting tense and expectant for half the evening, was a sharp intake of breath which might have been mistaken for a protracted hiss, a few seconds of stunned, disbelieving silence—and then, laughter, which screamed and echoed and multiplied round the theatre. It went on and on and on, it seemed as if it was never going to stop. When it threatened to die away, a fresh wave would burst out, louder and more frenzied than before. People rocked and shook and cried with hysteria. According to Stanley Bell's stop watch, it lasted a minute and a quarter, which may not seem much, but when it is considered that a big laugh in the theatre lasts on an average between ten and fifteen seconds, the *Pygmalion* laugh was unparalleled in theatrical history. 'People laughed so much,' said Mrs Pat afterwards, 'it nearly ruined the play.' After that, nothing could go wrong and nothing did. The audience which was clearly doting on every single minute of the play, screamed its approval so un-inhibitedly, that Shaw rose in disgust after the tea-party scene and stormed angrily out of the theatre. The news of Shaw's departure was quickly passed on to Tree while he was changing into his dress-suit for Act Four. 'Aaaaah, so the cat's away,' he said with a relieved smile, and then, knowing he was quite safe, proceeded to do everything Shaw had forbidden. At the end, the audience went mad with delight; Tree was quite openly crying and cut his usual curtain speech to the minimum, though he could not for-bear to mention Shaw's early departure. Then there were bouquets, flowers, endless curtain-calls, more speeches, tears and cheers and a cascade of roses thrown from the gallery. There were a few chords of dissent from the suffragettes in the gallery but these merely added spice to the occasion: no triumph is ever quite complete without a few boos. It was well past midnight before the happy but exhausted company were allowed to leave the stage and go up to the Dome where a first night party, complete with champagne, chicken and caviare, was held for them and a hundred of Tree's most intimate personal friends.

The following day there was a brisk exchange of telegrams between Shaw and Mrs Pat. 'MAGNIFICENT. SUPERB. NEVER BETTER' cabled Shaw. These were the first kind words she'd had from him for a long time and she was, understandably, very touched. 'YOUR GENEROUS PRAISE QUITE UNDESERVED' she replied. Even in his most tender moments, Shaw had no time for false modesty. He replied: 'DEAR STELLA. I WAS TALKING ABOUT THE PLAY.' But Mrs Pat was equal to this and her riposte was swift. 'DEAR JOEY. SO WAS I!'

'...It went on and on and on...'   *Daily Sketch*

7

OVER THE WEEKEND AND THROUGH-
out the subsequent week, the notices flowed in from
all over London and from every provincial city—
they were ecstatic. At enormous length and with a
wealth of plot-describing detail, the dramatic critics
—as fine a body of men as the metropolitan police,
in Max's phrase—wrote a series of what can only be
described as love letters to Tree, Mrs Pat, Shaw and
and His Majesty's Theatre. It was a hymn of joy, an
ocean of golden, glittering, heart-warming praise,
which brought long queues to the box-office and
relief to Number One dressing-room. This is where
the papers were delivered on the morning after a
first night, and it was Tree's special pleasure to call
there early in the morning and settle down for a
happy hour, plunging into the notices with either
approval or sadness. ' "Sir Herbert gives a splendidly
boisterous performance," ' he read out loud to Dana
and Bell, 'oh, how *very* kind, I did didn't I? . . .
"Sir Herbert's presentation of his phonetics professor was richly comic" . . . aaaah, yes it was wasn't
it? . . . "When Sir Herbert knows his lines, I shall
return and see this play again." ' He grimaced
sadly. 'How unkind. I really don't think that was
called for; oh, these critics, they just don't *understand* . . .' However, there was just one small detail
on which the critics were unable to agree. 'Sir Herbert is made up to an astonishing likeness to Lord

Northcliffe.' (*The Times*.) 'Sir Herbert contrives to resemble Mr Asquith.' (*Northern Echo*.) 'Sir Herbert looks exactly like Mr Winston Churchill.' (*The Observer*.)

Sir Herbert, in great agitation, takes refuge
on the piano.

But there was one point on which they were unanimous: the repetition of The Word by the snobbish suburban girl, Clara, did not amuse them.

CLARA: Such nonsense, all this Early Victorian prudery.
HIGGINS: (*tempting her*) Such damned nonsense.
CLARA: Such *bloody* nonsense (*exit laughing*).

Coming so soon after Mrs Pat had said it, the audience on the first night, it was rather gloatingly pointed out, had received it in silence. It was a pointless and inartistic repetition and upset the balance of the scene. Tree agreed and, knowing that Shaw had left London, told Margaret Bussé to cut it.

The story had broken, the secret was out and the headlines were now able to scream the good news to the tensely waiting world. BERNARD SHAW'S BOLD BAD WORD SPOKEN . . . MRS PAT UTTERS THE UNPRINTABLE SWEARWORD . . . SENSATION AT HIS MAJESTY'S . . . THE WORD REDUCES THE AUDIENCE TO CONVULSIONS . . . AUTHOR STORMS OUT OF THEATRE IN DISGUST . . . SHOULD WE PAY TO HEAR THIS DISGUSTING LANGUAGE? . . . UPROAR AT HIS MAJESTY'S . . . PROTEST BY DECENCY LEAGUE . . . THEATRE TO BE BOYCOTTED . . . I SEE NO OBJECTION SAYS PRIME MINISTER . . . SIR HERBERT CENSURED BY THEATRE ASSOCIATION . . . etc, etc, etc.

In those days when popular journalism had just come into its own with ten times as many papers as there are now, and unlimited time and space to spend on scandal and gossip, the newspaper coverage on *Pygmalion* exceeded even Tree's wildest dreams. Fleet Street and His Majesty's had always been on friendly terms, and never more so than in the early summer of 1914. Editors sharpened their pens and buckled down to work to supply a public greedy for sensation: what followed was an avalanche of rumour and denial, gossip, jokes, cartoons, letters, statements, interviews, leading articles, some of it sensible, most of it unspeakably idiotic, for the silly season began a little early that year. It was a tidal wave of newspaper lunacy which threatened to engulf everything in its path, for nothing else seemed to be happening during that last Edwardian summer.

'I certainly think The Word should be banned,' snarled the Bishop of Woolwich to an enterprising *Daily Sketch* reporter, 'it is disgusting and tasteless.' Other high-ranking church dignitaries fell over themselves to give their opinion. 'The Word is more *vulgar* than profane,' moaned Bishop Weldon, fluttering his long thin fingers nervously, 'I dislike vulgarity on the stage. It's not *nice*, not for an actress and in particular a married woman with children to have to speak the Word in public. As an effort at sensationalism I regard this as pretty cheap.' The Irish-born, David Dorritty, popularly known in Manchester as the Actors' Padre, flattered himself on his broadmindedness, as is the way of *padres* (as opposed to mere parsons), but even he could not bring himself to approve of The Word. 'If it were desirable to show a flower-girl reverting to type,' he said, chuckling heartily, his pipe clenched between manly, white teeth, hands deep in pockets, legs astride, 'then I think some milder expression might be used which would not give offence.' He took his pipe out and gazed at the reporter, his blue eyes blazing with sincerity. 'If I might make a suggestion, how about *not blooming likely?*' But it was the Reverend Waldron, Vicar of

Brixton who brought a note of sanity into these interviews. 'Shaw is out to interpret life,' he said, 'I don't
see how he could cut the Word. It is a great play
which mirrors life truly.'

The *Daily Express* was as resourceful then as it is
now. Acting on a casual suggestion from Tree, the
editor, R. D. Blumenfield, had resourcefully invited
a real flower-girl to see the first performance, all
expenses paid, in exchange for an exclusive interview afterwards. Their choice fell on one who sold
flowers in front of Charing Cross station and whose
name, by a strange coincidence, really was Eliza . . .
Mrs Eliza Keefe, aged thirty, married to a Covent
Garden porter and mother of six children. Her red
chubby cheeks, flashing cockney wit and warm-
hearted smile had made her well-known and well-
loved in the district over the fifteen years she had
worked there. Early in the morning of April 11th,
she had taken her place on a stool near the head of
the queue, and spent a whole day there, happily being
photographed and making many good friends in the
process. At seven o'clock she found herself sitting
in the middle of the front row of the pit stalls. After
the performance, two *Express* reporters took her to a
pub where, over several pints of milk stout, she gave
her candid opinion of the play.

Well [she said], I never had sich a night in all
me natural. Everybody a-looking at me and a-
photographing me and a-shaking me hand, and all
because I said as how I'd go and see how they

played a flower-girl in this play. You see, I never thought as how I'd be so conspic . . . well, you know what I mean. I thought I'd just sit in the queue, and then go and sit somewhere in the corner, see the play and then tell the bloke what I thought of it. Well, when we got into the theatre I found meself right in front of the pit. Then, when the nobs come in, all wearing evening dress, I got red in the face for they all turned round and stared at me. I could see some o' them was reading the paper with me picture in it and all, and when they saw the picture, they all turned round to have a squint at the real thing.

It was alright when the curtain went up, I reely enjoyed meself then, and when I heard the language, it was quite home-like. I never thought as how I'd hear sich words on the stage. I shall have a word or two to say about this before I've done. Now about Liza Doolittle, the flower-girl: I thought Mrs Patricia Campbell who played her was just *luvly*—but she was not altogether what you might call true ter life. As for Bernard Shaw, well, he thinks a blooming sight too much of himself, he does. There was one line in the first act which shows just how conceited he must be. It was when the Professor was talking about the flower-girl, when she was miserable at not being able to sell her flowers. 'The woman', says he, 'who can utter such disgusting sounds does not deserve to live anywhere.' When I heard this I could not help shouting 'R A T S' and people in

144

the pit says 'HUSH'. 'Hush yourself,' says I,
'he's got no right to say a thing like that.'

Now, I didn't like the bit when the prof. makes
his housekeeper take away the flower-girl's clothes
and burn them. It's as much as to say flower-girl's
are lousy. I thought Mrs Patricia Campbell talked
a bit rough. I asked people in the pit if I talked
as rough as her, and they said NO, not arf as
rough as her. I thought it was funny when she
got into the taxi wiv her basket. Of course, flower-
girls don't make a habit of getting into taxis, but
you know, when you've had a good day, you feels
sporty. I didn't like the last bit when Eliza's
supposed to fall in love with the Prof. He wanted
her to go back to him, yet he didn't say he loved
her. It wasn't one thing nor another. And then
Sir Herbert waves his arms round her, above her
and all over her, but he didn't kiss her or hug
her. Doesn't Mr Shaw believe in kissing or
hugging?

And now a bit about the language. There was
one word in particular which Mrs Patricia
Campbell said when she was supposed ter be a
lidy. The editor says I must not repeat it, but it
begins with a *B* and ends with a *Y*. WELL!! No
self-respecting flower-girl would say such a word
when she was on her best behaviour and speaking
in a drawing-room. And when another young lidy
said it after her, well, it sounded simply
horrible . . . I wish he'd found a better title.
Who's ter know *Pygmalion* is anyfing ter do wiv

flower-girls? It would have been better if he gave it a good rousing name like they have for the Lyceum dramas. He might have called it *From Flower Girl to Duchess* We should have known what it was about then. Mister Shaw can have this tip from me, free, gratis and fer nuffin.

The public was not slow to follow Mrs Keefe's example in giving their opinion of The Word. There is nothing more ludicrous than the British public suffering from one of its sporadic fits of morality; it can always be guaranteed to make a complete and utter fool of itself. This is precisely what happened. Shaw's Unmentionable Word ceased to be a matter of personal taste and quickly became a moral issue; the outbreak of outrage and indignation which filled the correspondence columns of the popular press sparked off the most virulent controversy of the season. 'Nothing could be more shocking and outrageous that the word Mr Shaw puts into the mouths of two innocent female characters,' wrote a Mrs Winifrid Stevens of Leinster Square, Bayswater, 'and even from an aesthetic point of view there can be no defence of such a gross outrage of good taste. If this blackguardly, foul-mouthed language is allowed to continue, it is an end not only to all decency and morality but to civilization as well. *We need no Billingsgate language in our drama today!*' 'I was appalled by the vulgar trash I heard in *Pygmalion*,' shuddered a Mr Collins of Wandsworth. 'Is it necessary to repeat all the spice one hears in life from the lower orders in order to make a play? Surely the clock is going back!'

A blast of anger came from Manchester. 'What is the theatre coming to when religion and all the things which honest, God-fearing people hold most dear, are traduced and mocked at,' roared a man from Chorlton-cum-Hardy, 'when evil is excused and idealized, and things are said and done on the stage which would never be tolerated in respectable circles. I am appalled to read that the utterance of this profane word not only passed without protest, but that the audience was convulsed with laughter. It is a proof of what a power for evil this clever and unscrupulous author can be, and an indication of the depths to which this particular writer for the stage has dragged the play-going public.' It was signed NOT A SHAVIAN.

'Ever since Mr Shaw flung his unprintable word at the play-going public,' wrote a sad little man in *The Sandwich Gazette*, 'my wife, who is a refined and educated woman, has regarded it as a huge joke to use this expletive on any and every occasion. When I protest, she retorts that society is treating it as a joke and that I have no sense of humour. May I ask whether one's sense of humour is likely to be still further strained, for there are many worse words used in the gutter which decent people have hitherto ignored.' 'What can have come over Sir Herbert Beerbohm Tree to put on such a play as *Pygmalion*?' snarled two energetic women from Scotland. 'It is vulgar. Had they not got so much respect for Mrs Patrick Campbell, half the audience would have hissed on Saturday night. Hardly five minutes go by without the use of objectionable language and disgusting swear-words. The majority of women do not wish to pay to hear these unspeakable expletives in the theatre—we hear quite enough of them at home!!' It was signed 'Two Late Admirers of Sir Herbert Beerbohm Tree.'

But an unexpected note of good sense came from a girl in Maidstone. 'Since Saturday morning I've been wondering what on earth was the word Mrs Pat was to speak and which it was quite impossible for your paper to print,' Patricia Woodlock, a twenty-year-old school-teacher wrote to the *Daily Sketch*. 'I had no idea of the harmless adjective which your mealy-mouthed writers found so distressing. What a stodgy provincial lot they must be. It's only in the backwoods of Manchester, Sheffield, Birmingham and Oldham that bores and stodgy puritans would protest and be what they call shocked. Be more careful of some of your writers, I'm sure they're too young and timid. Don't let them go to Shaw plays. Haven't you got a woman on the staff at Shoe Lane? The modern man is so very conventional, and it is so easy to rub the bloom from his pristine purity. I don't know what this expression means, but I've heard maudlin, sloppy men often use it about women.'

This provocative letter was immediately taken up by a very bad-tempered hotel-keeper in Wales. 'Miss Woodlock champions the use on the stage of one of the most senseless and offensive epithets in the English language, and condemns as puritans and bores those who have the courage to protest,' trumpeted George Shepherd of the Station Hotel, Cardiff. 'In my opinion she is contributing to Shaw's contemptuous attitude to women. During my management of hotels in Lancashire and Scotland, I have done my best to suppress this language and have refused time out of number to serve customers who have offended in this respect, even to the extent of ordering them off the premises. We all know Mr Shaw likes to be different—or likes to think he is—but his offence against the canons of good taste will be less easily forgotten than his unblushing piracy and theft of the garbage of Smollett.' 'I'm surprised that Mr Shepherd states that Shaw despises women,' retorted Patricia Woodlock, rushing to do battle. 'I don't understand this. Shaw today is woman's best friend, and he never—to use his own words—"treats us with reverence". He preaches the gospel of common sense and his women are jolly good company. The working classes lack imagination to invent swear words; their curses are so crude. Why doesn't some genuine friend of the working classes compile a manual of oaths? Some of the Italian ones are fine. They sound horrible, but they are really quite harmless.'

'Where was the Censor?' screamed the secretary of the Decency League from Brighton. 'Was this appalling word in the original script? If so, did it pass the Censor? If so, does he actually read the plays submitted to him? If not, then what is the use of him? It is doubtful if Mr Shaw has ever outraged good taste as he did on Saturday last. He has made light of the sacred rite of marriage, and has treated a distinguished and carefully selected audience to an outrageous sanguinary adjective. Nauseous and revolting realism cannot be excused when the standards of good taste should reign supreme.'

★

The moralists, having shot their various bolts and arrows, retired from the battle leaving it to the humorists, who proceeded to embark on a really glorious field-day. In musical comedies, concert-parties, revues and music-halls, the comedians jumped swiftly on to the band-waggon. A profusion of songs and sketches were written and endless jokes were made about Shaw, Mrs Pat, Beerbohm Tree and His Majesty's. *'What the Bernard Shaw are you doing?' 'It's all my eye and Mrs Pat'* and *'Not Pygmalion Likely'* became popular catchphrases of the day, guaranteed to bring a howl of delight to audiences ready and eager to seize on a topical reference. At the Alhambra Theatre, George Grossmith presented a new revue whose title *Not ****** Likely* enlivened the posters up and down the Strand; *The Passing Show*, a revue at the Palace Theatre, introduced a short sketch *Not Vermilion Likely* in which Mr Arthur Playfair as a very niminy-piminy Higgins, recited:

'Sir Herbert Tree
Exclaimed "Dear me!
Must I return my thanks?

        Reporters dog
            My dialogue
        With asterisks and blanks." '

And Mr Nelson Keys, as a bass-voiced Eliza in a
long black gown and tiara, answered:

        'Oh, Sir Herbert, I'm no ham
        my language may be ruddy;
        I'm very tired of *blast* and *damn*
        It's really very ******'

the asterisks being filled in with a bass note on the
trombone, and at the Shaftesbury where the musical
comedy, *The Pearl Girl*, was playing, the star, Laurie
de Frees, hastily inserted a new song in which a
theatre-going bishop is reproved by an attendant for
attempting to see the new Shaw play:

        'You're in the wrong department,
            Don't stay here any more.
        It's evident you do not know
            This play's by Bernard Shaw.
        His Language is so very bad
            He's not content with "D", sir.
                As you may guess
                His gross excess
                Has vastly shocked
                The daily press.
                He'll now be known as
                    G.*B*.S.
        With the accent on the "*B*", sir.'

(*Punch*)

All over the country, in stately homes, castles and London drawing-rooms, at banquets, receptions and dinner parties, the younger generation struggled to free itself from the restraints imposed by their seniors. Jazz, socialism and fast cars for the men; make-up and smoking for the women, these were the last nails in the coffin of Victorian prudery. The Word was the final thud of the hammer, and the gilded Edwardian youth, who were tired of 'beastly' and bored with 'awfully', gleefully used 'bloody' up and down the town, tumbling over each other to introduce the word into polite conversation. Let their elders storm and protest, let them thunder and denounce, let them ask questions in the House or write letters to *The Times*—it didn't matter. Mrs Patrick Campbell, a respectable married woman with two children was saying it every night with the full consent of the Lord

Chamberlain in a theatre dedicated to and named after His Britannic Majesty, King Edward the Seventh. She was saying it under the auspices of an actor-manager knighted by the late King whose multiple relations were queuing for the seats in the Royal Box. All this represented the highest possible hallmark of social respectability which none, surely, could gainsay. The Lord Chief Justice and the Archbishop of Canterbury saw the play and were seen to be laughing immoderately, thus adding legal and ecclesiastical blessings to Royal approval; and when the Cardinal Delegate from Rome and the Archbishop of Westminster, having conferred on themselves the necessary dispensation, filled the stage box with their purple and scarlet magnificence, it was felt that this Papal benediction had placed the matter beyond doubt or argument. The Word had come to stay and had been found acceptable by the highest in the land. *Nihil obstat. Imprimatur.*

The *Daily Sketch*'s forecast had been an accurate one: The Word *did* become the catchword of the season, and not only in the houses of the aristocracy —the middle classes, following eagerly on the heels of their social superiors, took up The Word joyfully. In suburban and provincial drawing-rooms all the way from Dulwich to Dundee, The Word was freely used and tolerated. 'The other day I was driving down the Haymarket,' wrote a man in the *Morning Post*, 'when my taxi happened to collide with another in front. *"Take care, you bloody fool,"* shouted my driver. I was about to speak to him most severely when I looked up and there I saw His Majesty's Theatre. What Bernard Shaw writes, you can hardly blame a cabman for saying.' In South Africa, the case of a white woman who called a Johannesburg policeman a bloody fool and was charged with using obscene language, was dismissed by the magistrate who said: 'Bernard Shaw has shown in his new play that the word is used by polite society in England.'

In the rarified columns of *The Times*, the *Westminster Gazette* and the *Cambridge Review*, a lengthy correspondence started in which university dons, classical scholars and other assorted intellectuals eagerly discussed the true meaning and derivation of The Word. Was it, as many supposed, a corruption of 'by the blood of Our Lady', which made it blasphemous? Or did it merely stem from the ancient Nordic word '*bløde*', meaning 'to have carnal knowledge'? in which case it was merely obscene. A new novel was published which, anticipating Billy Liar's father, contrived to use The Word seventy-nine times in its 400 pages. 'I grew tired of counting it,' said one literary critic. The book was quickly snapped up by Mudies and Harrods Libraries, and swiftly banned from the Army and Navy Library services, since innocent soldiers and sailors, as all well knew, had never heard or used The Word and must at all costs be protected. A correspondent in the *Leicester Post* invited members of London high society to visit Leicester if they wished to learn how best to make use of the forbidden Word. 'Let them study the conversation in a taproom in a Belgrave Gate public-house, or better still spend a Saturday afternoon on the popular side of our local football grounds. They would then learn how to introduce this lurid word at least half a dozen times in a single sentence.' The Oxford Union solemnly debated 'This House approves the use and acceptance of a certain sanguinary expletive as a sign of a liberating influence on the English language' and then voted unanimously in favour of the motion; while the boys of the Eton Debating Society discussed 'This House deplores the debasement and vulgarization of the commercial theatre' before solemnly starting rehearsals for a school production of *Macbeth*. Members of The Womens Purity League held a meeting at the Central Hall, Westminster and then delivered a letter of protest to Number Ten, Downing Street. The newspapers continued to be coy about reprinting the dreadful word in their sacred pages, referring primly to it as '------' (*Morning Post*), as 'b----y' (*The Times*), 'this sanguinary expression' (*Observer*), 'the universal epithet of Billingsgate' (*Daily Mail*), 'an expletive which good taste will not permit us to mention in these columns' (*Chronicle*) or 'an adjective which Mr Kipling tells us every recruit learns to say "with every word he says"' (*Sketch*). The only publications which dared to print it in full were the *Westminster Gazette* and the *Church Times*.

The effect of all this was immediate and predictable. The public clamoured for tickets, the first month was sold out within two days, and long queues formed daily at the box-office, stretching down the

Haymarket and well into Pall Mall. Even Tree was unable to get seats for his friends and was compelled to go to the ticket libraries. It was all too good to be true but Tree was still not entirely convinced that Shaw's handling of the production was yielding the desired result, and was forced to pay daily visits to the box-office to reassure himself that all was well. Even so, there were some unexpected pockets of opposition. The Theatre Managers Association wrote a sharply worded letter of protest begging Tree to withdraw the unseemly word, their members having complained that they stood in danger of having their theatre licences withdrawn. Tree was highly incensed by this, and refused to answer it himself, delegating this unsavoury task to Dana who informed the Association that no changes could be made without the author's authority, and he very much doubted if this would be given. He was, theirs truly . . .

The author, meanwhile, had fled from London to escape all this nonsense. Peace and solitude were essential if he was to recover from the nervous strain of the last two months. He had just seen a set of photographs taken after the première which made him look like an old dog who'd been caught in a fight and got the worst of it. He was so appalled that he refused to allow them to be published but he did send a set to Tree and Mrs Pat with a brief inscription: 'This is *your* doing!' He embarked on a lengthy walking tour of Yorkshire, this being his favourite form of relaxation, but even so he could not escape the press and he was eventually traced by two enterprising reporters to the Queen's Hotel, Filey, where he was coaxed into making a statement. 'I did not think the critics would have written with such a feeling of resentment,' he said, 'there are always a number of people protesting against something they consider to be indelicate. The word has been used on the stage—there is nothing new in it. Shakespeare uses it in *Macbeth* and other plays. It need not give the slightest offence if it is used artistically and sincerely. In my opinion, the fuss is due to affectation and incapacity of intellect. I'm sorry if certain people's feelings have been hurt, but they are in a hopeless minority. After all, if they don't like the play, they can always stay away from the theatre.' The *Clydebank Gazette*, noting that Shaw was in York-shire, suggested that his next play might well be set there. 'If he wishes to use even wilder expletives or horrid phrases with all the stops out, then he has gone to the very best part of England. Nowhere can the language be more appalling to unaccustomed ears than in Yorkshire whose natives habitually employ the most disgusting expressions.' The *Clydebank Gazette*, it might be noted here, was published in an office near the Gorbals in Glasgow.

Sydney Grundy now entered the fray. He was the author of a number of light comedies which had enjoyed a considerable success back in the nineties, and Shaw during his critical years, had been particularly unkind to them. After twenty years the memory of all those humiliating outbursts of Shavian wit still rankled; now the position was reversed and Grundy seized this heaven-sent opportunity of paying back an old score. 'Although there is no harm in Shaw's incarnadined adverb when informed by genius,' he wrote, 'from Shaw's pen it is poison. Shaw is imperilling the liberty of the English theatre. Public opinion is gathering storm over this deeply resented outrage.' Public opinion demonstrated the full extent of this outrage by filling the theatre at every performance and screaming with delight. A week after the première, a rumour started that Tree was going to bow before the storm and cut The Word. This naturally produced a further stampede at the box-office with outraged theatregoers falling over themselves to be still further outraged while there was time. Nothing could have been further from the truth: the rumour had been cleverly planted by Tree who proceeded to give his own remarkably sensible views on the subject to the press in a conference held in the Dome. 'Mrs Campbell uttered the word at today's matinée and nobody was shocked,' he announced calmly, 'the only reasons for the press reports being so vehement is the flatness of the political situation. The Word was passed by the Lord Chamberlain and there my responsibility ends. There is nothing blasphemous or obscene about The Word. It may be found in the works of Rudyard Kipling and John Masefield. It may not be good taste for ladies of gentility to wear gaudy feathers in their hats, but they are not obliged to follow Eliza Doolittle's taste and example either in this or in the matter of the Word. Besides,' he added smiling at the long line of scribbling reporters, 'I would like to add that a Word which is generally applied to Queen Mary Tudor should not be censored in a flower-girl.'

Shaw returned to Adelphi Terrace at the end of April and was immediately pestered by reporters begging for a further statement about the play. 'It's my *As You Like It*' he said, 'which means as the public likes it. But I must tell you very firmly that it is N O T as I like it.'

★

It seemed that all was not well at His Majesty's theatre, and this was entirely due to the eccentricities of its manager. Tree was one of those irritating actors who never really know their lines until a couple of weeks after the first performance. During this period, his excitable imagination was able to roam, eagerly experimenting with new ideas, new intonations, bits of funny business, new touches of character. He was congenitally incapable of repeating a performance—'you know, repetition is so *boring*', he would moan, 'it's the death of true acting; when a performance is fixed, it ceases to live.' Acting on the impulse in a series of entirely spontaneous ideas could produce some extraordinarily effective moments, but he was incapable of producing these effects every night; that is where technique takes over from inspiration, and Tree had no technique. For example, his first performance of Higgins was a mess but very funny; his second was much tidier but rather dull; his third was very good throughout except for a few shaky moments, and his fourth was very bad. When he had finally succeeded in learning the part he promptly lost all interest in it, and this was the danger-point as his company and playwrights well knew. Then he would wearily devise new and more outrageous bits of business, make funny faces at the other actors, play practical jokes on them—he was an ardent practical-joker—put in topical references, anything to keep boredom at bay.

> Come soon, [wrote Mrs Pat to Shaw on
> April 17th], or you'll not recognize your play. I
> hope you make £40 ordinary nights and £80
> Wednesday and Saturday—then perhaps you can
> accept the mushy show with some sort of toler-
> ance . . . Tree takes 5 minutes between each
> word and each bite of the apple in Act 4. I have
> facial paralysis trying to express some sort of
> intelligent feeling, so now I hide my face until
> it is well again.

Also, there was the irresistible urge to improve on the author, which he had done many times before and believed he could do again. The critics and public had hailed his Malvolio and Falstaff as being improvements on Shakespeare, his Svengali was much more striking than du Maurier's rather woebegone creature and his Micawber funnier than in Dickens. Here was his opportunity to demonstrate that he could make Higgins a much more fascinating character than the rather commonplace bachelor whom Shaw had forced on him. In Tree's estimation, this meant one thing—

romance. Now that Shaw was safely in Yorkshire, he could do what he had always wanted to do, and show that Higgins was really deeply in love with Eliza. This he did by doing the very thing which Shaw had expressly forbidden; throwing flowers to Eliza in that brief interval which occurs between the end of the play and the fall of the curtain, clapping his hands with joy and blowing kisses to her.

It was a good example of Tree's basic childishness that in spite of all this he wanted Shaw's approval of his performance, and typical of his naïvety that he imagined that he would get it. 'Tree has only one ambition,' said Mrs Pat to Shaw, 'that you should be pleased with his Higgins.' Shaw's complete lack of interest in his performance and in the play after it had been launched, was a source of considerable irritation to Tree, who considered that it was the natural and inescapable duty of the author to be in regular attendance. 'Wilde, Jones, du Maurier and Haddon Chambers came every night,' he said reproachfully to Shaw one day when they met at the Club, 'I can't imagine why you don't. Aren't you interested? Besides, there are a number of little things I've thought of which I'd like you to see.' He pestered Shaw with such persistence that he eventually relented, promising to come to the hundredth performance. 'That, of course, is the equivalent to not coming at all,' added Shaw unkindly. The hundredth performance was finally reached and survived and Shaw was compelled to redeem his promise. What he saw fully lived up to his worst fears:

Tree had contributed a number of inventions of such grotesque and outrageous irrelevance that Shaw solemnly cursed the whole enterprise and refused to set foot in the theatre again. Once again Tree was unable to understand this, and with the bewildered innocence of a small boy, he reproached his difficult author. 'My ending makes money, you ought to be grateful,' he said. 'Sir Herbert,' trumpeted Shaw, 'your ending makes nonsense, you ought to be shot.'

Though she might complain about Tree's acting, Mrs Pat's own performance as Eliza was just as unpredictable and variable. If she was in a bad mood, if she had a headache or felt tired, if she had been irritated by something or somebody, or if she just didn't feel like it, then she wouldn't bother to act and had, apparently, no qualms about giving her adoring public short measure. Monday nights were bad, she had never liked Mondays. Matinées, particularly hot sunny Wednesday ones, were worse, she really hated matinées, even though she was paid extra. Although she never actually missed a performance, on these occasions she certainly never gave a good one. Then she would walk through the play, bored, listless, frequently inaudible, killing her own laughs and everybody else's, upstaging the other actors, shifting the furniture to suit herself, and even, during one very hot matinée, talking to friends in the stage box while Tree and Merivale were playing a scene in the first act.

The only occasions when she took good care to be at her best were when royalty was present, for she was a terrible snob. There was, after all, always the possibility of a Presentation in the Interval and an invitation to supper afterwards at the Palace or Embassy. There was always—who knows—the possibility that she might be honoured for her services to the theatre, though the question of her name presented certain problems: Dame Patrick Campbell was a little ambiguous, but Dame Stella Campbell had a definite ring to it. This innocent little weakness was widely known and secretly laughed at amongst her friends and admirers: connoisseurs of Mrs Pat-manship, before booking their own tickets, got into the habit of consulting the Court Circular to see who else was going. Her love of royalty was one of the few absolutely genuine emotions she possessed: and her curtsey, which was a miracle of grace and elegance, was the ritual through which this fervent adoration found its true expression. There was a very large network of English and inter-related continental royalty during the summer of 1914, so both Mrs Pat and her adoring public did well out of it.

Queen Alexandra and the Empress of Russia enjoyed your play mightily, [she wrote to Shaw], and clapped and nodded with joy.

Your play *goes* every night most wonderfully. But Tree's performance is a most original and entertaining affair . . . Mine is a mere masquerade! You are no shepherd, or you would have taken more care of your fold . . . You must come again Joey dear. I am nervous about my part F. G. Smith and Sheldon said they liked my *pathos* best—best thing in the play!! God knows what maudlin stuff I have let into the part.

And so that long, final, Edwardian season ran its glittering, dazzling course; long hot summer days merged smoothly into long warm summer nights. At His Majesty's there were long queues in the day, House Full boards displayed in the evening, and champagne parties in the Dome at night. Week after glorious week flowed smoothly past bringing £130 a week to Mrs Pat, £280 a week to Shaw and over £2,000 to the theatre. Constable's brought out their green-backed acting edition and requests to stage the play flowed in from all over the Continent, from Russia, Japan and South America. Not that the season passed entirely without unfortunate incident: Mrs Pat was compelled to take to her bed for a week with severe headaches and stomach cramps, and her place was taken by Elsie Mackay; and Carlotta Addison suddenly died in the middle of June aged 65. Her performance as the sad, socially insecure Mrs Eynesford-Hill mourning her genteel poverty in Earls Court, provided the play with its most touching and moving scene, and her death was widely mourned by the profession. Her place was taken by Edmund Gurney's wife, Alma Murray.

In the meantime, Tree was getting desperately bored with the play and cursing each day he had to spend in it. 'This horrible, relentless success,' he moaned, 'it's killing me. Oh, damnation to Art.'

When July brought a prolonged heatwave he could stand it no longer and promptly withdrew it. It had run for three months and had made a clear profit of £13,000; he could have made much more if he had been interested in money, but now he was more interested in a holiday, so at the beginning of August he and the family went abroad to Marienbad.

'It is quite absurd that the notice should go up at the end of a £2,000 week,' complained Mrs Pat as she and George set off for a short fishing holiday in Ireland. She asked Shaw if she could take over the entire production under her own management to fill in the gap before their departure for America. 'Alexander is willing to let me have the St James's,' she wrote, 'and we can move the play there at once at the end of the fortnight putting in the people I want for America. You will do a little work with them, for me won't you—and with me too? I stand to make £600 a week for you in America so you must help me. What about Norman Trevor for Higgins? Tree will have to be approached very tactfully. I can have the St James's the 21st of September and then I can have three weeks, and then off to America . . . Have you any objection to my taking *Pygmalion* to a few big towns in September?'

On the very same day on which Mrs Pat was writing this letter, an ominous and momentous event was taking place in Bosnia. An Archduke whom nobody had ever heard of was assassinated in an obscure little town whose name nobody could pronounce. Within a few weeks, all Europe was in flames. Tree was compelled to rush back from Marienbad and Mrs Pat and George from Ireland. The projected English tour was indefinitely postponed and the season at the St James's was cancelled. The First World War had begun.

ELIZA'S HAT

Eliza's hat under discussion
by Sir Herbert and
Mr. Merivale.

8

THE POSSIBILITY OF TAKING
Pygmalion to America had been under discussion as
far back as March 24th when New York's German
Theatre in Irving Place gave the American première.
The topsy-turveyness of the situation, an English
play by an Irish author performed in German for an
American audience, did not stop the New York producers, many of whom were Germans themselves,
from attending in full force. It was not good;
Rudolf Christian had directed it as a broad farce, the
translation did scant justice to Shaw's subtleties and
from the only existing production photograph it
could be seen that Doolittle emerges in his Act Two
as a truly bizarre figure unlike any English dustman
before or since—a neatly-pressed boiler suit, shiny
pointed shoes, wide-brimmed artist's hat and a
volume of Oscar Wilde's poems peeping out of his
pocket.

After the His Majesty's première, Lee Shubert
offered Mrs Pat $1,500 weekly to play Eliza in New
York but he wanted an American cast to support her.
Naturally, she refused, and it was Theodore Liebler,
who eventually persuaded her. He was more than a
mere producer; he was an *impresario*. Unlike most
of the others he had discrimination and taste. He
was the Sol Hurok of his day who specialized in
importing foreign star actresses to New York—Duse,
Rejane and Bernhardt had all come under his

banner. He was charming, handsome and cultured: he was a European and he spoke her language—money, and plenty of it. He invited Mrs Pat to bring her London company, and he offered the unheard-of sum of $2,000 a week.

When the war started, she refused to come. George Cornwallis-West and Beo both joined up in the Scots Guards and for two months she stayed miserably in London anxious to help the war effort and cursing her own uselessness. It was Shaw who convinced her that she was far better off playing *Pygmalion* in America than worrying herself into a breakdown over her menfolk in the trenches. She cabled her acceptance to Liebler giving him barely a fortnight for preparation and at the beginning of October, she and her company left England for what finally proved to be an absence of eighteen months. She had tactfully invited Tree to come with her but he had clearly had enough of Mrs Pat, of *Pygmalion* and of Higgins which he had no desire to play under her management. With the war rumbling away in the background, he was entirely preoccupied with revivals of *Drake's Drum*, *Henry IV* and *David Copperfield* which ran through Christmas and well into the New Year. The projected production of *Treasure Island* was never referred to again and was allowed to sink without a trace into the archives of the theatre.

Now, at long last, Mrs Pat had the opportunity of doing what, from the first, she had always wanted—presenting the play under her own management, directing the rehearsals herself with a little help from Shaw and the stage-manager, and with a company of her own choice. In the absence of Tree she selected Philip Merivale, that charming, polished actor who had played Colonel Pickering with such fine breeding and discretion, that a certain critic was moved to comment that the Colonel was the only true gentleman whom Shaw had ever created. Merivale was a sensible choice for her and for the play. He was an excellent actor, completely reliable and fully professional both in execution and in attitude; he was one who could give her the loyal support she so badly needed without ever outshining her, a salaried employee whom she could keep in the background and act off the stage and who, tactfully and self-effacingly, could supply her with the romantic hero, which, in open defiance of Shaw's intentions, she had always wanted.

There were two other members of the original company—Algernon Greig who played Freddie and the indispensable Edmund Gurney. Otherwise the company, which had been drawn from a profession already sadly depleted by the frenzies of wartime recruiting, was hurriedly assembled and hastily rehearsed. They opened on October 12th at the Park Theatre on 59th Street, a much smaller building than His Majesty's for which the specially constructed scenery had been prepared.

After the first performance she wrote to Shaw·
The hot weather tired the public—last night they came and the play went gloriously. Don't believe

any paper that says I am sentimental. I'm *quite*
simple—years too old—I *can* be heard . . . I
have had the grippe—the doctors attended me—I
missed no performances.

The production was very cramped and unfinished
and received mixed notices. 'The performances by
these London actors were adequate and will seem
still more so when they have had a few more rehearsals,' said the *Brooklyn Eagle* sardonically. 'Mrs

"I'm one of the undeserving poor," says
Mr. Edmund Gurney as Alfred Doolittle.

170

Campbell seemed sure of her lines, Philip Merivale is a charming personality, but it is the actor Edmund Gurney as the windy Doolittle who gives the finest performance of the evening. The others listened intelligently to their principals, and occasionally to the prompter.'

It didn't matter. Nothing mattered as long as Mrs Pat was in the cast. This was her fourth visit to America and she had a large and adoring public. In spite of mixed notices, *Pygmalion* was a huge and triumphant success. The Americans loved Shaw and were not in the least bit shocked by The Word, regarding it as a charming and delightful piece of English slang. In New York, as in London, it spread like wildfire through the fashionable drawing-rooms of Park Avenue and was eagerly quoted by everyone, the old and conservative as well as the young and fashionable.

The *New York Times* electrified its readers by boldly announcing that Shaw was at last going to pay his first visit to America but a cablegram of Shavian wrath soon crushed this piece of wishful thinking. 'It would not be fair to the American press: for twenty years they have filled any spare room in their columns by announcing that I was on my way to America, thereby keeping the public under a strain to which they are not accustomed. If I were to disappoint everybody by actually coming at last I should create a lot of ill-feeling. Besides, nobody would go to see *Pygmalion*, they would all come to see me.' Once again, Mrs Pat had the last word. She sent him a card, 'From all appearances your play is a great success; you are a made man.'

Shaw knew that once she was safely in America and he was unable to keep a strict eye on her, she would shamelessly take advantage of the fact and would bully and fascinate George Tyler, the manager, into letting her do what she pleased with the play, particularly with reference to cuts in the text which he knew she wanted. In a witty and perceptive letter, Shaw warned the man of the danger he was in.

You'll find Mrs Campbell's changes of dress will take longer than the changes of scenery [he wrote in October], the play is very hard work for her on this account, and you will please arrange dressing-room accommodation in such a position as to avoid running up and down the stairs. If you cannot give her a room on stage level, she will agitate for a tent (she had one at His Majesty's here); and when she starts agitating, don't argue but surrender at once, even if it involves rebuilding the theatre. In the long run, you'll find this cheaper.

When you have fixed her up comfortably in this respect you can press her if necessary to keep pace with the stage-staff. If she does that, the play can be got through between 8 and 11. Tree got through it by 11.30; and Merivale can easily save half an hour on Tree if the others keep going. You must be firm about this; for Mrs Campbell wants to cut the play, partly because

its length hurries her dressing and interferes with
the delightful levées she holds in her dressing-
room, and partly because she thinks that Mrs
Pearce and Doolittle are insufferable bores and
should be cut down to two or three lines apiece.
She has already told me that you want the play
cut by half an hour; that New York people will
not stay so long in a theatre; that she will not
play the last scene to empty benches, etc, etc, etc.

You must agree with her in all that and deplore
my pigheadedness in insisting on the whole play
without a word omitted. It is no use arguing; she
is clever enough to talk your hair grey; but she
has no more judgement than a baby, and will
spoil the play if you let her. She does not know
where the interest of the play really comes; and
does not care twopence about the part to which
she has never given five minutes' serious thought,
except as an excuse for fascinating and a joke; and
unless she is forced to be serious and kept hard
at work, she may quite possibly get on the wrong
side of the public with the play, and let it drop
through when everybody is tired of the scandal of
her saying 'Not bloody likely'—which, by the
way, unless it is said with perfect unconsciousness
and sincerity will wreck the play on the first
night. She can give a charming performance if she
likes, and if she sticks loyally to the text and does
not gag or play for silly laughs. The worst of it is
she doesn't like, and, as I have said, is not really
interested in the entrails of the play but only in

its superficial effectiveness which soon becomes tedious.

The moral of all this is, that, for her sake and your own, you must stick to me and to the play and resist all her wiles to have it cut down (which wouldn't save a moment of time; for she'd waste all you saved) that is, *if* mortal man can resist such a siren—which I rather doubt.

Naturally, the public knew nothing of all this. The unique, the irresistible, the irreplaceable Mrs Pat was once more in their midst and that was enough. She found herself a legend and all she had to do was to live up to it. The press kept an eager, watchful eye on her; everything she did, however trivial, made news—her arrival on the Lusitania smuggling the heavily doped Pinky-Panky-Poo through the customs in a hatbox, the purchase of two more animals to keep him company, a Japanese sleeve dog called Pooh-Pooh and a chinchilla Peke called Woosh-Woosh, her sensational beginner's luck at bridge when she won $25,000 in a single evening.

For the last time, America opened its loving arms wide. It was her greatest personal triumph there; she was lionized and pursued and flattered as never before. She charged and received $100 for a newspaper interview, cash strictly in advance, though this didn't guarantee results for the one boring question she could not endure was 'What do you think of America?'; also she hated being addressed as Mrs Pat and disliked people to think she was a Scotswoman. One unlucky reporter who fell foul of her on all three points provoked a predictably stormy reply. 'You'd better interview Pooh-Pooh!' she shouted as she rushed from the room. 'He'll give you his candid opinion of America with pleasure.' Park Avenue Hostesses queued up to give her parties, millionaires placed cars and Pullman trains at her disposal, she was a weekend guest at the White House.

The supreme accolade came when she complained of insomnia, which inspired her ever-resourceful press-agent, Jules Worms, to pull off one of his greatest publicity stunts. He went to the City Cleaning Department and persuaded them to deal with the matter. 'Her contract with us says that she has to be sent back to England in good health,' he said, 'and if she breaks down because she can't sleep, she'll sue us for every buck we have.' The Department thus ordered that the entire length of 43rd street outside her hotel be covered with tanbark to muffle the noise of the traffic; streetcars were ordered to slow down and silence their bells, news-boys were told to stop shouting, policemen wore rubber soles, organ-grinders were banished to another street and, to complete the picture, according to a cynical report from the *New York Times*, 'bar-tenders were persuaded to use a specially muffled ice when shaking their cocktails.' No other actress had ever thus been honoured, and it produced some strange and unaccountable rumblings of jealousy from other American actresses. Otherwis ethere was, perhaps, only one person in the whole of New York who was not completely enchanted by her presence in the big city, and that was an anonymous Brooklyn taxi-driver who was privileged to escort her and Pinky-Panky-Poo to the theatre one evening. It was as she was alighting from the taxi that the driver's eagle eye spotted evidence on the floor of a certain small misbehaviour. He let out a scream of anger and pointed an accusing finger at the wretched pekinese. Mrs Pat gathered Pinky-Panky-Poo into her voluminous bosom and looked scornfully at the driver. 'Nonsense, my good man,' she boomed for all Broadway to hear, '*it was me*!'

There was another myth-making incident which was destined to have very far-reaching consequences. If America was unmoved by Eliza Doolittle's bad language, they were horribly shocked by Mrs Pat's habit of smoking in public, which was then severely frowned on, America being considerably behind England when it came to female emancipation. One day she was sitting in the tea-room of the Plaza Hotel and the manager saw that she was smoking. Cowering behind a pillar, for he was mortally afraid of her, he sent a waiter to deal with her. 'Please madame, you must not smoke here,' the waiter said nervously, 'it is not permitted, please, no.' Mrs Pat fixed her famous basilisk stare on the wretched man. 'Young man,' she trumpeted for all the Plaza Hotel to hear, 'I have been told that this is a free country and I don't mind telling you that this is the only thing about America which I do not wish to alter!' Next day the papers were full of it and the gilded salons of Park Avenue buzzed with the scandal. Then Mrs Clinton Fiske, leading New York hostess and self-appointed arbiter of social morality, gave her opinion. Speaking for all American womanhood, she said, 'In my opinion, for a woman to smoke in public is not only unfeminine, it is positively *un-American.*' As a result of this, smoking was later banned in the New York subway for everybody. It still is, and Mrs Pat was responsible.

The press hung on her lightest word, the most trivial remark was reported. 'American actors cannot speak Shakespeare, they sound like *taxi-drivers.*' 'American men look splendid, but what a pity they have to open their mouths.' 'Americans are not reflective nor retrospective—just prospective.' 'American parties are so *noisy,* like the French revolution.' But she didn't always have the last word. During the final dress-rehearsal at the Park Theatre, there was some dispute between her and Liebler. 'Mr Liebler, I wish you to understand quite clearly that I am a professional actress.' Liebler's reply was swift. 'Thank you, madame, I promise I'll keep your secret.'

The New York custom of transferring plays rapidly from one theatre to another was a source of considerable annoyance to her. 'It's like hide-and-seek,' she moaned after the fourth transfer. 'Nobody will know where we are, it's the best kept secret in New York.' Nevertheless, the play ran successfully to capacity business through the autumn, past Christmas and well into the New Year. 'A man sent me quite a nice notice of *Pygmalion* the other day,' wrote Shaw. 'It reads as if you were really beginning to move people in Eliza.' Later, in January, he wrote, 'I have just received the returns for your Xmas week. Ruin is retrieved by four mammoth performances in two days. It's funny how steadily it averages out at £1,500 a week. Are they overworking you?'

After the New Year, she revived *The Second Mrs Tanqueray* and gave a series of performances in repertoire with *Pygmalion*. *Mrs Tanqueray* had had several revivals in New York, the film had been widely seen and the play had been done to death by all the stock and touring companies; nevertheless, Americans were very anxious to see her in her most famous part. She was, admittedly, twenty years older; the Tanqueradiance had dimmed a little, but American theatre lovers decided that Mrs Pat as Paula, even if she was past her prime, was still eminently worth seeing, far more so than any other actress at her best.

After four months she closed her season at the end of January and took the two plays on a long and exhausting coast-to-coast tour which carried her and the company up and down the entire length and breadth of the North American continent. 'Oh Joey,' she said later when remembering the fatigue and strain of those endless months, 'when I was young I was a *tour de force*, but now that I'm old I'm forced to tour.' This was the point at which George Cornwallis-West sailed out to join her having been in-

valided out of the army. Life with Stella had turned
out to be a somewhat greater strain than he had
anticipated and he hadn't exactly relished being
called (as, alas, he was) Mister Patrick Campbell.
But if it had been difficult to live with her, it proved
to be impossible to live without her, and after a
separation of six months he was eager for a reunion.
The problem of what to do with him was solved
when he announced a long-suppressed desire to act
and asked if a part could be found for him. By a
happy coincidence, Edmund Gurney was due to
leave the company to take up some very lucrative
and attractive offers from Broadway and Hollywood producers, his success having made him very
much in demand. Mrs Pat gave the part of Doolittle
to her husband and coached him with loving care.
To everybody's astonishment he was passably good
and played it with a modest success for the next three
months; 'as good as Gurney,' was Mrs Pat's proud
verdict. Shaw greeted this with polite scepticism,
merely remarking acidly to a friend that he had
always suspected that Doolittle was a completely
actor-proof part and that this was the final confirma-
tion of it.

In San Francisco, the public didn't know how to
pronounce the title, choosing to call it 'Pigma-*Lion*'
and imagining that it had some vague connection
with *Androcles and the Lion*. Since no one in the play
actually says the title, San Francisco, much to its
disappointment, remained in ignorance as to its
true pronunciation.

Joey dear [wrote Mrs Pat from Chicago in February], it's quite dreadful, 6 more or less nice letters from you to me—and not one from me to you . . . There's no excuse excepting the hard work of the tour—and three severe colds and a cough and three doctors and a nurse and two nights off—and more than once 9 performances a week and the last week in New York, *eleven* performances, ten of *Tanqueray* . . . and eight of *Pygmalion* . . . I like Merivale's playing of Higgins immensely—it's so *alive*—He adores you and is faithful to all you said . . . I am thinner and I don't look dreadfully old for the part.—Still it would be better if I were 25 years younger—if only you'd write the play I want! but you can't and won't try!

George continued to play Doolittle and Orreyd in *Tanqueray* quite adequately, but the unaccustomed strain of acting and company-managing on tour produced a brain storm and a nervous breakdown. He retired to Colorado Springs for a holiday and then returned to London.

By the end of 1915 she had played Eliza everywhere and even America's appetite for the combination of Shaw and Mrs Pat had been satiated. Business began to drop and the royalty statements which fluttered every week into Shaw's flat in Adelphi Terrace told their own sinister story.

The returns from Newark have given me an irresistible opportunity to preach [he wrote on

December 19th]. I don't know what sort of place
Newark is; but when it comes to houses of thirty
pounds it is time to look for a new play . . .
Enormously successful plays like *Pygmalion* are
the most dangerous plays in the world. Nine
times out of ten they are run on till every farthing
they have made is lost again. That is what will
happen to you with *Pygmalion* unless you stop in
time. If you cannot find a new play, then go and
live in a cottage until you do find one; it will be
cheaper than losing money at the rate *Pygmalion*
will lose it once it begins to fall down hill. There
is also the loss of prestige: all the New York
people—the Shuberts and Klaws and Erlangers
and the rest—know what business you are doing,
and value you accordingly.

★

She returned to London in 1916 and made several
attempts to revive *Pygmalion* in the West End.
Alexander was approached and considered the
matter. 'I think *very little persuasion* and Sir George A.
will do *Pygmalion*', she wrote to Shaw who evidently
had other ideas and his own methods of spiking her
guns. 'I don't know what you have said to Alexander
but it has effectively put him off doing *Pygmalion*', she
complained. A provincial tour under Charles Macdona's management was projected. In April 1917 she
wrote: 'I don't think it would harm *Pygmalion* to be
played for 12 weeks with the 4th Act omitted and a

few lines cut,' she suggested hopefully, but Shaw evidently thought it would, so while Shaw, Mrs Pat and Macdona haggled about percentages and royalties, the tour was abandoned.

It was Tree who expressed a definite desire to revive the play. He had spent the war years touring his gorgeously mounted productions of Shakespeare round the grateful American continent, and now in 1917 he was wholly preoccupied with war relief, writing and delivering speeches, arranging meetings and producing charity performances. He and Shaw were present at a Royal Academy of Dramatic Art conference, their first meeting for three years. Tree was in good form, brimming over with fun and vitality; never had his childish good humour and wit bubbled more delightfully. He made Shaw feel like his grandfather, hopelessly old and grumpy. As they walked away down Gower Street, he discussed a possible revival of *Pygmalion* as if it promised to be a renewal of the most delightful experience of their lives.

The following week, while on holiday in Kent, he slipped down stairs and fractured his knee-cap. He returned to London and Sir Alfred Fripp performed a minor operation. Tree recovered quickly and then proceeded to enjoy a hilariously sociable convalescence, surrounded by visitors, and making tremendous plans for the future. One evening he was having his dinner in bed on a tray; the night nurse was peeling a pear for him. At his request she went to close the window; his head suddenly fell back on the pillow and when she turned to him, he was dead. It was horribly sudden and pointless, but he died as he had lived, happy, radiant and laughing. Tree was the last of the great actor-managers and the Edwardian Theatre, that golden, glittering extravagant age, which survived the death of King Edward by six years, can be said to have died with him. 'The friendliest, most enthusiastic, most hospitable and the most infuriating of creatures,' said Mrs Pat after the funeral. 'He was the despair of authors,' added Shaw. But the angel of death was not to be so easily satisfied. A few months later Beo Campbell was killed in the trenches in France. Beo, her handsome, charming, spoiled, irrepressible son, was the one person in the world she truly and unselfishly loved. Once again it was to Shaw that she confided her agony and from his outburst of rough, angry, commonsensical sympathy that she derived some grain of comfort.

★

It was Viola Tree who carried on her father's good work by going into management in 1920 and presenting Mrs Pat in her first West End revival of *Pygmalion*, at a ruinous salary of £1,000 per week. She had a very distinguished cast to support her—Marion Terry as Mrs Higgins, Robert Andrews as Freddie and C. Aubrey Smith as Higgins; time had swiftly brought its revenge, for having spurned Smith in 1914, she now found that he was the only actor of any stature who was willing to act with her.

He was a kindly man, but pompous and without humour, which brought out the devil in her and she teased him mercilessly as she had done with Alexander. 'Good morning, Aubrey, *dear*,' she would trumpet as she made her usual late entrance at rehearsals, 'have you brought your cricket bat with you?'

Rehearsals were even more chaotic in 1920 than they had been in 1914. The whole production had been arranged in a great hurry and Shaw found that he had only three weeks to rehearse the play. Aubrey Smith had great trouble remembering his lines and took frequent time off to appear in a film. The casting of the smaller parts was careless and haphazard and in the last week, Edmund Gurney was cabled to rush back to London from New York and fit himself into the completed production with what he could remember of Doolittle. But Gurney was playing Richard Barthelmess's father in the D. W. Griffith film, *Tol'able David*, for ten times the money Viola Tree could afford to pay him, so the part was given to Frank Bertram. Viola Tree, though a charming and delightful person who was greatly loved by everybody, kept up the family tradition by being hopelessly unprofessional as a theatrical manageress. 'She is a spoiled child playing with dolls,' wrote Shaw to Mrs Pat 'she declares that Marion Terry's movements are so beautiful that she must keep walking about the stage, which means that there is going to be a beauty and youth contest between Mrs Higgins and Eliza.'

It opened at the Aldwych rather prematurely on February 10th, 1920 to excellent notices. The production was a mess: Aubrey Smith continued to be unsure of his lines and Mrs Pat, with her youth and beauty and figure rapidly vanishing, was a great disappointment to those who had seen her before as Eliza and an object of disbelief and ridicule to the younger generation who had not. She wore terrible dresses and insisted on too much front lighting on her face which made it look like a kitchen clock and flattened her figure to twice her natural size. 'She played Eliza like Mrs Cornwallis-West in a very ill tempered and brazen mood,' said Shaw, but even he admitted that in the third act she could still give the world a lesson in comedy acting. It transferred to the Duke of York's in May with Frank Celler taking over Higgins for C. Aubrey Smith, and it was there that Shaw saw it for the second time.

You have now got the play as nearly . . . as you ever will get it [he wrote to her]. You are very much better than you were when I saw it before on the first night at the Aldwych . . . You have got rid of that horrible third act dress; and though the fifth act dress is dramatically non-sensical, yet as you now really do act a bit, and relate yourself to Eliza, you are quite credible *as* Eliza . . .

You now play the second act and the fifth act so very cleverly and nicely that I damned you up hill and down dale for doing it so badly for *me* when you could do it so well for yourself. It is now really good Victorian drawing-room drama, pleasant and sweet, and in what you (bless you!) call good taste. You are not a great actress in a big play . . . but you have your heart's desire, and are very charming . . . I enjoyed it and appreciated it in its little way. And that was magnanimous of me, considering how I missed the big bones of my play, its fortissimos, its allegros, its precipitous moments, its contrasts, and all its big bits. My orchestration was feeble on the cottage piano; and my cymbals were rather disappointing on the cups and saucers. Still, you were happy; and that was something. And Higgins was not brutal to you, as I was. A perfect gentleman.

Still, you have lost as well as gained. The fourth act was a failure. You really might have given me a turn there with advantage. You looked like the loveliest of picture postcards blinking there at the piano whilst Higgins was talking daggers—'Thank God it's over'—'the whole thing has been a bore' etc, etc, etc.—without turning a hair, making your eyes twinkle like stars all the time—no shadows, no spasms, no stabs of pain, nothing but Stella. How carefully you avoided hurting him with the slippers; and how tenderly he raised you and reciprocated your gentleness! I almost slept . . .

The receipts, by the way, are so appalling that I doubt if the public knows that the play is on again. Or did Aubrey make all that difference?

If so, let's turn our faces to the wall, and die. A procession of sandwich men might help; but we can't afford them.

Later in the year, after a disastrous appearance in a very bad play about George Sand by Philip Moeller, she took *Pygmalion* to Germany and presented it to the British Army of Occupation. The authorities could not afford to pay her anything like her West End salary, but it was a highly enjoyable busman's holiday with expenses paid and the reassuring knowledge that she was helping the war effort. During this fortnight she played to thousands of soldiers who had never seen her, never seen a Shaw play and never been inside a theatre. She was, as she herself described it, 'over-praised, over-entertained, over-photographed', but it was fitting that her farewell to *Pygmalion* should have been with a bang rather than a whimper. She was never to play Eliza again. Age and increasing weight had caught up with her to the point where she could not get away with it, not even with all her skill and her charm and her genius. Since that first performance in 1914 she had given more than seven hundred performances of Eliza and had travelled over thirty thousand miles to give them, and now, at the age of fifty-five, it was the end.

Two years later she wrote her memoirs, *A Life and some Letters*—more letters than life, it turned out, and not many of these, for there had been a lot of trouble over them. Shaw, on whom she had concentrated her hopes, bluntly refused her permission to publish any of his. 'No, Stella, NO, it's absolutely out of the question,' he shouted when the subject came up, 'I have not the slightest intention of playing the horse to your Lady Godiva!' Since Hutchinson's had advanced her £2,000 on the expectation of them, she was in an unfortunate position; when it was made clear that she would either have to refund the money or be taken to court, he generously relented and allowed some carefully edited, quite innocuous letters of his to appear in the final manuscript to justify his name in the publicity. The book was published early in 1922, and did unexpectedly well, bringing in total receipts of £2,500. It is not good. Apart from the occasional amusing passage, the revealing glimpse, the odd, happy turn of phrase, the book is dull, badly-written and snobbish. It reproduces end-less press-cuttings and flattering letters from literary and theatrical celebrities and contrives to say very little about its authoress. Its interest lies more in what is omitted rather than what is included; she was in a bad temper with Shaw when she was writing it; she says almost nothing about *Pygmalion* and the little she does say is both distorted and malicious.

In his play *Pygmalion*, he succeeded in making me exclaim '*bloody*' nightly before a thousand people—he thought to conquer my pre-Raphaelite instinct. I invented a Cockney accent and created a human Eliza Doolittle and because the last act of the play did not travel across the footlights with as clear a dramatic sequence as the preceding four acts—owing entirely to the fault of the author —he declared that I might be able to play a tune with one finger, but a full orchestral score was Greek to me . . . . Later, he wrote the end of the story of 'Eliza Doolittle' and when he found I had not read it, he sent me the following letter:— 'There are four depths of illiteracy, each deeper than the one before:

1) The illiteracy of Sir Henry Irving.
2) The illiteracy of those illiterate enough not to know that he was illiterate.
3) The illiteracy of those who have never read my works.
4) The illiteracy of Eliza Doolittle who couldn't even read the end of her own story.

There is only one person who is such a Monster of Illiteracy as to combine these four illiteracies in her single brain. And I, the greatest living Master of Letters, made a Perfect Spectacle of myself with her, before all Europe.—G.B.S.'

But as usual it was Shaw who had the final word. When she suggested yet another revival of *Pygmalion* in 1923 (he refused to allow it) he looked up and down at her with ferocious cynicism. 'Good God, Stella,' he roared, 'you're forty years too old to play Eliza—but if you sit still and don't move a muscle— *maybe nobody will notice ! !'*

Index

Addison, Carlotta 51, 86, 164
Admiral Guinea 49–50
Aix-les-Bains 37
A Life and Some Letters 187
Albert Hall 36
Aldwych Theatre 185
Alexander, Sir George 13, 14, 18, 20–2, 31–2, 37, 40, 42, 44–5, 90, 123–4, 165, 181
Andrews, Robert 183
Androcles and the Lion 179
An Enemy of the People 94
A Midsummer Night's Dream 81
Apple Cart, The 14
Archbishop of Canterbury 9, 153
Archbishop of Westminster 153
Arms and the Man 16
Asche, Oscar 119
Ashwell, Lena 35
As You Like It 159
Asquith, Anthony 3, 140
Asquith, The Rt Hon. Herbert 140

Back to Methuselah 14
Barthelmess, Richard 184
Beerbohm, Max 139
Beethoven 46, 47, 76
Beeton, Mr 12
Belasco, David 19, 100
Bell, Stanley 57, 66, 68, 71, 72, 85, 110, 137
Bella Donna 11, 18–20, 22, 24, 37
Bellew, Alfred 71
Bennett, Arnold 119
'Beo' (Alan Campbell) 18, 38, 183

Bernhardt, Sarah 9, 10, 38
Bertram, Frank 184
Blenkinsop, Dr 81
Billy Liar 154
Blumenfield, R. D. 143
Boise, Harriet 41
Braithwaite, Lilian 119
Brayton, Lily 119
British Actors Equity Association 101
Britomart, Lady 2
Brooklyn Eagle, the 176
Buchanan, Jack 119
Buchel, Charles 122
Bussé, Margaret 51, 86, 141
Byron, Lord 9

Caesar and Cleopatra 8
Caligula 72
Calthrop, Donald 119
Cambridge Review, The 154
Campbell, Alan ('Beo') 18, 38, 183
Campbell, Helen 38
Campbell, Mr Patrick 12, 13, 73
Campbell, Mrs Patrick: her death 1; refusal to play in *Pygmalion* film 2–4; birth and background 10–11; marriage 12; début at St James's 13; meeting with Shaw 17; love affair with him 28–36; taxi accident 36–9; behaviour at *Pygmalion* rehearsals 70–5, 85–90, 102–3; second marriage 104–9; first night performance 135–8; and subsequently 162–3; American

tour 167–81; 1920 revival of *Pygmalion*, 183–6; memoirs 188–9

Campbell, Stella Patrick 18, 38, 95

Carpentier, Georges 120

Carson, Sir Edward 120

Cellier, Frank 185

César, Franck 72

Chambers, Haddon 161

Chaminade 72

Chaucer 20

Chesterton, G. K. 110

Chopin 72

Christian, Rudolf 167

Church Times, The 155

Churchill, Lady Randolph 105–6

Churchill, Winston 105, 113, 114, 120, 140

Cleopatra 16, 94, 96

Clydebank Gazette, The 157

Craven, Alfred 134

Constable (publisher) 164

Copperfield, David 97

Coquelin 10

Cornwallis-West, George 105, 106, 109, 165, 166, 167, 178, 180

Court Theatre 8, 49

Daily Express 98, 143

Daily Mail 155

Daily Sketch 124, 126–8, 153, 155

Daily Telegraph 74, 136

Dana, Henry 49, 50, 57–8, 68, 77–8, 85, 89, 90, 92, 139, 156

Darling of the Gods, The 100–1

Dean, Basil 104, 108, 110

Delisse, Irene 51

Devil's Disciple, The 18

Doctor's Dilemma, The 16, 18, 81, 94

Don Quixote 44

Dorritty, David 142

Dorset Arms Hotel, East Grinstead 106

Dowager Empress of Japan 120

Drake's Drum 167

Drew, John 33

Drinkwater, John 91

Dubedat, Mrs 16, 94

Durieux, Tilla 41

Edward VII 153, 183

Elliott, Maxine 94

Empress of Russia 163

Erlanger 181

Eton Debating Society 55

Expiation 46–7

False Gods 93

Falstaff 43, 160

Fanny's First Play 8

Fechter 60

Fiske, Mrs Clinton 177

Forbes-Robertson, Sir Johnston 8, 16, 81, 123–4

Frees, Laurie de 151

Fripp, Sir Alfred 37, 182

Frohmann, Charles 32

Gaiety Theatre 64

Galatea 98

Garrick Club 56–7, 90, 96, 108

Gaskill, Mr 12

George V 9, 100, 120

German Theatre, New York 167

Getting Married 18

Gilbert, W. S. 20, 50–1

Grainger, Percy 124

Granville-Barker, Harley 8, 51, 70, 119
Great Adventure, The 119
Greig, Algernon 86, 169
Greenroom Club 96, 108
Griffith, D. W. 184
Grossmith, George 150
Grundy, Sydney 157–8
Guinness, Benjamin 1
Gurney, Edmund 51, 72, 81–3, 112, 136, 164, 169–71, 179, 184
Gwenn, Edmund 33

Hamlet 16, 73
Hawkesley, Bouchier 106
Haymarket, Theatre Royal 43
Heartbreak House 14
Hedda Gabbler 11, 18, 94, 95
Helen of Troy 60
Henry IV 43, 160, 167
Hichens, Robert 18
Hiller, Wendy 4
Hofburgtheater, Vienna 41, 113
Hooligan, The 49, 50
Howard, Leslie 3
Hutchinson (publisher) 5, 188

Ibsen 18, 94
Iris 14
Irving, Sir Henry 30, 33, 55, 60, 124, 189
Irving, H. B. 40, 123

Johnson, Jack 120
Jones, Henry Arthur 25, 161

Kaiser, The 9
Kean, Edmund 60
Keefe, Mrs Eliza 143–6
Keen on Waller Society 40
Kendal, Mr 12
Kendal, Mrs 33

Kipling 158
Kismet 119
Klaw 181
Keys, Nelson 151

Lady Godiva 188
Lady Macbeth 11
Land of Promise 119
Lang, Matheson 40, 119
Leicester Post 154–5
Lessing Theatre, Berlin 41
Liebler, Theodore 167, 177
Lloyd George 82
Loftus, Cissie 36
Löhr, Marie 3
London County Council 63, 113
Long John Silver 77
Loraine, Robert 24, 30–1, 33, 35–6
Lord Chamberlain 8, 44
Lord Chief Justice 153
Lusitania, The 174
Lyceum 16, 56, 124
Lyttleton, Dame Edith ('D.D.') 24, 25, 27

Macbeth 49, 155, 157
Macdona, Charles 181–2
Mackay, Elsie 108, 164
Macready 60
Madame Sans-Gene 23
Magda 11
Major Barbara 2
Malvolio 76, 160
Man and Superman 18, 31
Martin-Harvey, Sir John 124
Masefield, John 158
Maugham, W. Somerset 119
Maurier, George du 160, 161
Maurier, Gerald du 39
Merivale, Philip 51, 72, 73, 102, 162, 169, 171–2, 180

Melville, Harald 122
Micawber 160
Mitchell, George 120
Mixed Grill 119
Moeller, Philip 187
Moisewitch, Benno 120
Moonbeam 23
Moore, Mary 31
Morning Post, The 153, 155
Mrs Warren's Profession 16
Mr Wu 119
Murray, Alma 164
My Fair Lady 63

Nathans 71
National Film Company 97
Neilson, Julia 31
Nero 76
Newcombe, Colonel 76
News Chronicle 16
New York Times 171, 175
Northern Echo 140
Northcliffe, Lord 97, 140
Notorious, Mrs Ebbsmith, The 11

Observer, The 155
Oliffe, Geraldine 51
Opera Arcade 71
Ophelia 10, 16
Orinthia 14
Oxford Union 155
Ozonair, Ltd 125, 126

Pall Mall Gazette 114
Pankhurst, Mrs 2
Park Theatre, New York 177
Parker, Louis N. 46
Parsons, Alan 108
Parsons, Denys 100
Pascal, Gabriel 3
Passing Show, The 150
Patti, Adelia 20
Pearl Girl, The 151

Peregrine Pickle 20–1
Phelps, Samuel 60
Pinero 13–15, 51
Pinkie and the Fairies 77–8
Pinky-Panky-Poo 108, 174, 176
Plautus 20
Playfair, Arthur 150
Plaza Hotel, New York 176
Poel, William 51
Pooh-Pooh 174–5
Pope, The 9
Price, Nancy 22
Pro Patria 106
Puccini 19
Pygmalion (film) 2

Queen Alexandra 163
Queen Mary 100, 120
Queens Hotel, Filey 157

Rehan, Ada 33
Réjane 9
Robertson, Graham 77
Royal Academy of Dramatic Art 182
Royal Dramatic Theatre, Stockholm 41

Saint Joan 81, 91
Sandow 32
Sardou, Victorien 19
Sargent 91
Saturday Review, The 16, 43
Savoy Theatre 8
Second Mrs Tanqueray, The 11, 13, 40, 48, 178, 180
Shaw, Bernard: position before 1914 5–9; meets Mrs Pat 17; reads *Pygmalion* to her 23–6; his infatuation over her 27–36; *Pygmalion* produced abroad 41; reads it to Tree 48–50; directs rehearsals 55–

90; *Observer* interview 110–13; Final Orders to Mrs Pat 115–18; recuperates in Yorkshire 156–7; second glimpse of *Pygmalion* 161–2; directs 1920 revival 183–7
Shaw, Mrs Charlotte 4, 34, 36
Sibelius 124
Siddons, Mr 12
Shepherd, George 149
Shewing Up of Blanco Posnet, The 8, 44, 45, 50
Shubert, Lee 167, 181
Slater, Oscar 120
Smith, C. Aubrey 40, 183–6
Smollett 20–1
St James's Theatre 13, 15, 21, 37, 40, 56, 165
St George's Hospital 37
Stracey, Sir Edward and Lady 37
Sullivan, Barry 30, 60
Svengali 160

Tearle, Godfrey 119
Terry, Edward 30
Terry, Ellen 5, 9, 22, 24, 28–31, 124
Terry, Marion 183–4
Tesman 94
Theatre Managers Association 156
Thesiger, Ernest 81
Thoughts and Afterthoughts, 62, 124
The Times 98, 106, 140, 152, 154, 155
Tol'able David 184
Treasure Island 77–8
Trebell, Alfred 133
Tree, Sir Herbert Beerbohm: friendship with Shaw 42–5; accepts *Pygmalion* 48–50; at

rehearsal 55–70, 75–90; table-talk at the Garrick Club 90–6; final rehearsals 96–103; first night 129–38; behaviour during the run 159–66; his death in 1917 182–3
Tree, David 100, 101
Tree, Felicity 44
Tree, Iris 44
Tree, Lady Maud 44
Tree, Viola 100, 183
Trevelyan, Hilda 33
Trevor, Norman 165
Trilby 62, 85
Tyler, George C. 172

Vanbrugh, Irene 31, 90, 119
Vaudeville Theatre 33
Vedrenne-Barker 8
Voltaire 20

Wagner, Richard 124
Waldron, The Reverend 142
Waller, Lewis 40
Waynefleet, Lady Cicely 94
Weller, Tony 115
Wells, H. G. 110
Westminster Gazette 154, 155
Westminster, Shelagh, Duchess of 105
Wheldon, Bishop 142
Wilde, Oscar 12, 161
Wood, Sir Henry 120
Woodlock, Patricia 148–9
Woolwich, Bishop of 142
Worms, Jules 175
Woosh-Woosh 174
Wyndham, Sir Charles 31, 123
Wyndhams Theatre 56

Zakkuri 76, 100
Zapata 120

About the Author

RICHARD HUGGETT was born in London, educated at Ampleforth
and St. Paul's and trained at the Central School of Drama. He
has performed at the Royalty Theatre in London with the Lunts,
at the Comédie Française, in Covent Garden, and has traveled
extensively in the theatre. His own acting version of "The First
Night of *Pygmalion*" was an overwhelming success at the 1968
Edinburgh Festival.